MEDJU

Medjugorje:

Religion, Politics, and Violence in Rural Bosnia

Mart Bax

VU Uitgeverij
Amsterdam, 1995

Anthropological Studies, Volume 16, in cooperation with CentRePol

VU University Press is an imprint of:

VU Boekhandel/Uitgeverij bv
De Boelelaan 1105
1081 HV Amsterdam
The Netherlands

tel.   +31(0)20 6444355
fax   +31(0)20 6462719

isbn   90-5383-384-6
nugi   653

Layout: Sjoukje Rienks, Amsterdam
Cover design: Auke Bender, Amsterdam
Edited by: Vallauri Crawford, Volcano, Hawaii
Maps: BRON, Amsterdam

To Janny, Jeroen, Arjan and Menno

Contents

Acknowledgements

Several chapters or parts of chapters have seen the light of day in earlier versions. For the purpose of this book, they have all been recast and rewritten, extended and updated. A major section of Chapter Two was published under the title 'The Madonna of Medjugorje: Religious Rivalry and the Formation of a Devotional Movement in Yugoslavia' in *Anthropological Quarterly* 62 (2), 1990: 63-76. Substantial parts of Chapters Three, Six, and Seven were published as articles in *Ethnologia Europaea*, respectively under the titles 'The Seers of Medjugorje: Professionalization and Management Problems in a Pilgrimage Centre' (*E.E.* 20, 1990: 167-176), 'How the Mountain Became Sacred: The Politics of Sacralization in a Former Yugoslav Community' (*E.E.* 22, 1992: 115-125), and 'The Saints of Gomila: Ritual and Violence in a Yugoslav Peasant Community' (*E.E.* 22, 1992: 17-31). Chapter Five is a revised version of 'Women's Madness in Medjugorje: Between Devils and Pilgrims in a Yugoslav Devotional Centre', which was published in *The Journal of Mediterranean Studies* 2 (1), 1992: 42-54.

In the process of writing I have been helped and stimulated by comments, suggestions and constructive criticism from Vlado Bačić, F.G. Bailey, Karin Bijker, Bill Christian, Ger Duijzings, Joop Goudsblom, Caroline Hanken, Petar Jelećanin, Ed Koster, Daan Meijers, M. Estellie Smith, Fred Spier, Bonno Thoden van Velzen, Kitty Verrips, Sjef Vissers, Alex Weingrod, Ineke van Wetering, Eric Wolf and Cas Wouters.

My informants in Bosnia, Hercegovina, and various Croatian communities abroad provided hospitality and multifarious help. For reasons of safety I will not mention them by name. Many of them are also *personae dramatis* in this book; therefore, I use fictitious names only.

Several Franciscan communities in ex-Yugoslavia and elsewhere in Europe kindly gave me permission to do research in their archives. So did Dr. Marek Zurowski, keeper of the records of *Kirche in Not* in Germany.

Sheila Gogol made sure that my original Dutch texts were properly translated into English; she also edited my English texts.

Sjoukje Rienks kindly typed the manuscript and also processed the final draft.

My wife, Janny, and my three sons, Jeroen, Arjan and Menno, encouraged me before and after field work and stimulated me in writing. I dedicate this book to them.

I am grateful for all the assistance provided.

Note on Names and Pronunciations

Where 'Bosnia' is used as a geographical term, it means the whole territory of modern Bosnia and Hercegovina.

The pronunciation of Croat is regular and simple. The following important differences should be observed:

c	is pronounced as	'ts'	(as in bats)
č	"	"	"	'ch'	(as in chair)
ć	"	"	"	'tj'	(as in future)
dj	"	"	"	'j'	(as in journey)
j	"	"	"	'y'	(as in yard)
š	"	"	"	'sh'	(as in shadow)
ž	"	"	"	'zh'	(as in treasure)

Prologue

'It is like layers of an onion, and the more you peel them away, the more you feel like crying'. (James Miller, ex-MI5 agent)

This book is the result of more than a decade of research in Medjugorje, a peasant village in the southeast of Hercegovina. Ever since 1983, I have spent a number of weeks there every year. Even in the war years of 1992, 1993 and 1994, I was able to visit the region, though it was not easy or without danger.

My data are mainly based upon participant observation and in-depth interviews with the local population. In addition, the archives of the parish, several Franciscan monasteries, and regional newspapers were valuable sources of information. Politicians and government officials in Čitluk and Mostar provided me with useful data, as did several local historians and novelists. I also studied numerous pamphlets and booklets printed by devotional movements. In the past ten years, books on the phenomenon of Medjugorje have been published throughout the Western world, and I think I have read most of them. Lastly, I consulted social scientific and historical publications on (ex-)Yugoslavia, which are listed in the Bibliography.

Medjugorje became a pilgrimage centre in 1981, the year the Virgin Mary allegedly appeared to a group of local children. Via these children, Mary is said to have summoned the people of Medjugorje, the citizens of what is now ex-Yugoslavia, and indeed the entire world to seek repentance, atonement and peace. Since then, the seers—young adults by now—say they have been receiving daily messages and instructions from *Gospa* (the Lady), as they call the Virgin Mary.

Medjugorje was soon widely renowned, and pilgrims arrived from far and wide. According to local estimates, by 1990 there had been more than eighteen million of them. It was in that year that religious tourism collapsed and things became quiet in Medjugorje. The Peace Centre, as the site is called, turned into a hotbed. The rapidly crumbling state monopoly over the organized means of violence made it possible for old local family feuds to erupt into open hostilities fought out with a great deal of bloodshed. When the 'great war' had yet to start in Bosnia Hercegovina (April 1992), Medjugorje's 'little war' had already been fought—completely unobserved by the pilgrimage circuit. When the gunpowder had settled and the pilgrimage was hesitantly resumed, it was only in the eyes of the pilgrims that everything seemed the same as before.

My interest in Medjugorje was not roused by personal religious considerations. Nor does this book fit into the mainstream of pilgrimage literature, which highlights the 'mystical events', and the pilgrims' moods and motivations but almost overlooks the trials and tribulations of the local population.[1]

For me, Medjugorje was initially little more than a test case for a theory I had developed in a long-term research project called 'The Power of the Roman Catholic Church in Rural Dutch Brabant'.[2] The aim of this political anthropology project was to describe and explain the genesis and evolution of religious regimes in that part of Dutch society. The term 'regime' was coined to indicate configurations of human beings linked to each other in terms of control and dependency.[3] The Roman Catholic Church could thus be analyzed as constellations of regimes and subregimes, and more easily compared with secular regimes such as 'local authorities' and 'the state', which religious regimes are related to in many respects. In short, religious regime formation and processes of state formation and state development were central to the project, which aimed to bring together 'religion' and 'politics', two fields of anthropological inquiry that had drifted apart.

In the course of the research, it became evident that throughout the larger part of the nineteenth century, rural Brabant had been confronted with a veritable multitude of saintly apparitions, mostly local saints, each of whom became the focus of an important local devotion and pilgrimage supervised by a local monastery. A preliminary analysis demonstrated that this development coincided with the establishment of a diocesan organization in the area. Subsequent systematic archival research showed this was no coincidence: the local devotions appeared to be instruments of power in the battle between local, monastically dominated religious regimes and the diocesan regime, the parochial administration being the major 'prize'. By 'putting up a saint' and stimulating devotion to him or her, the local monasteries, which had administered most of the rural Brabant parishes up to then, were trying to maintain that power base and prevent diocesan encapsulation.

Medjugorje seemed to be an interesting case for the further testing and refining of the theory. A university colleague drew my attention to the 'case of Medjugorje', cursorily linked in ecclesiastical circles of the time to an old 'intra-church dispute'. Franciscan priests in the area were defying the episcopal authority, or so it was said. They refused to transfer the parishes in the region, which they had administered for centuries, to the diocesan priests to be appointed by the Bishop of Mostar Duvno. Apparitions of the Virgin Mary, according to certain ecclesiastical sources, were being exploited by the Franciscans to bring this intra-church dispute into the open, and to obstruct the episcopal pursuit of diocesan encapsulation.

My field work in the region, as well as among emigre Franciscan friars and laymen elsewhere in Europe, produced so many fascinating facts that, for the time being, I decided to exchange rural Dutch Brabant for Medjugorje. Since then, I have made one or more lengthy scientific 'pilgrimages' to Medjugorje every year. A major quest of the research, and a central question in this book, has been to discover what happens to the population of an ordinary, out-of-the-way peasant village when it becomes a devotional focus for millions of people from all over the world.

When I launched this project more than a decade ago, I could not imagine I had alighted in 'volcanic territory' where eruptions of human violence were the rule rather than the exception. As time passed, it gradually became clear to me that this was a region 'where the most primitive branches of the Serb and Croat tribes live' (Glenny 1992: 140). Blood vengeance, vendettas and other forms of private justice were 'normal' phenomena that regularly recurred and barely seemed to be alleviated by the pacifying activities of either church or state. Once the area was darkened by the shadow of the great war in Bosnia Hercegovina, in retrospect it was only logical. Thus a study initiated to test a theory on a religious phenomenon increasingly addressed the many-sided interdependency of what we are accustomed to refer to in terms of separate compartments like 'religion', 'politics', and 'violence'.

This book is not an ethnographic community study in the usual sense. Readers will not find any chapters on 'kinship, descent and marriage', 'making a living', or 'social stratification'. Nor will they be presented with a special 'historical background' chapter. This does not mean information of that kind is not important and has been omitted; it is simply approached from a different angle. The chapters can be read like essays in an anthology covering aspects of Medjugorje but at the same time addressing topics and problems of wider relevance. Yet the book is more than a collection of essays. The sequence of the chapters reflects the developmental dynamics of the social configuration of Medjugorje. Marian apparitions linked to intra-religious competition (Chapter Two) have evoked friction between the seers and the priests in charge of the devotion, who were thus confronted with management problems, which are in turn the subject of Chapter Three. The rapidly growing number of pilgrims has caused new kinds of inequality among the local population. This has fostered the emergence of new patronage networks (Chapter Four), stimulated protest behaviour on the part of the local women (Chapter Five), revitalized latent antagonisms among the clans and hamlets of the parish (Chapters Six and Seven), and so on.

The sequence of the chapters also parallels the researcher's own process of gathering data and insight. It involves the reader more closely in the exploratory expedition of anthropological field work. Each successive chapter presents a new aspect and also shifts back in time, shedding new light on earlier information and clarifying hitherto unsolved problems. The Marian apparitions, or so it appeared in time, not only had to do with intra-church discord, but also with long-standing disputes and conflicts among segments of the local population. In the course of the research, it became increasingly clear that these local disputes constitute a vital clue for a proper understanding of Medjugorje's development. This is clearly reflected in the course of the chapters, in which violence, particularly intra-village violence, becomes ever more prominent. It culminates toward the end of the book, when the pilgrimage centre is ravaged by a 'total war'.

The critical reader might question the relevance of such a detailed description of one small rural community in a remote corner of Bosnia Hercegovina. More specifically, what can we learn from this case study about present-day problems in that part of Eastern Europe? In *The Civilizing Process* (1982), Norbert Elias repeatedly noted that social developments are characterized by a combination of regularity and randomness, explainability and pure chance. On lower levels of integration, occurrences that might be regular and explainable on a high level become erratic, unpredictable, and dependent on random circumstances and personal quirks. Ever since the Middle Ages, the processes of state formation and state development in Western Europe have exhibited regularity and structure, development in a certain direction, and can be analyzed and interpreted as such. It is from this perspective, characteristic of Western Europe, that the developments in former Yugoslavia in general and in Bosnia Hercegovina in particular are generally examined and evaluated, using terms like erratic, irrational, pointless and inconsistent. My analysis of Medjugorje shows that what might seem random and unpredictable on a higher societal level demonstrates a large extent of regularity and explainability on a local level. The conclusion seems obvious that for a better comprehension of the present-day problems in Bosnia Hercegovina, attention should be more intensely and systematically devoted to processes and developments on the lower levels of social integration.

Lastly, a few comments to more religiously involved readers. Let me emphasize that I do not make any statements whatsoever about the 'truth' or 'authenticity' of the apparitions and the related religious phenomena and practices. Nor do I in any way address the issue of the integrity of the individuals involved. Problems of this nature do not lie within the framework of social science research.

Notes to Prologue

1. Some recent exceptions to this dominant trend are: Eade and Sallnow (1991), Kselman (1978), McKevitt (1988), and Zimdars-Swartz (1991).
2. Cf. Bax 1983a, 1983b, 1985, 1987 and 1992. See also Wolf 1991.
3. See Bax (1987) and Wolf (1991).

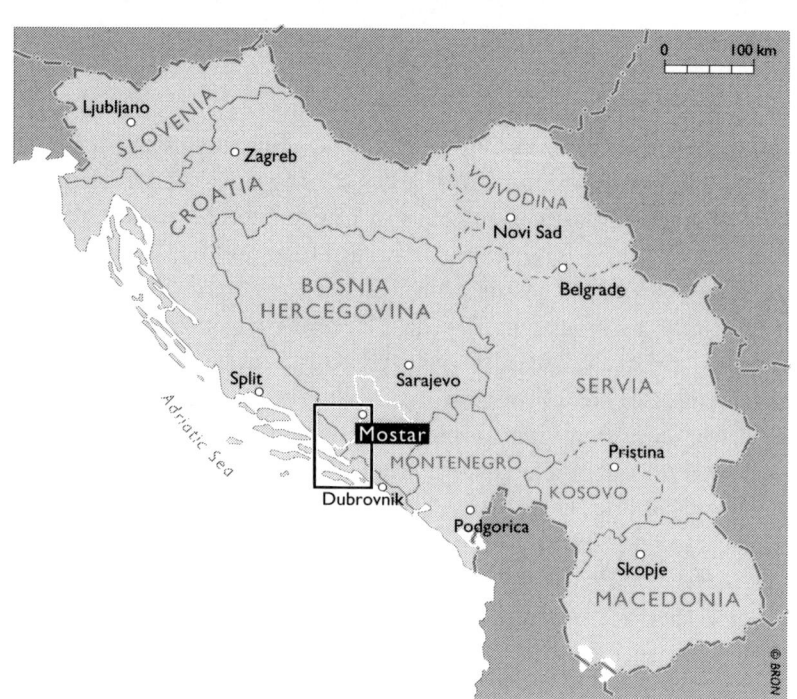

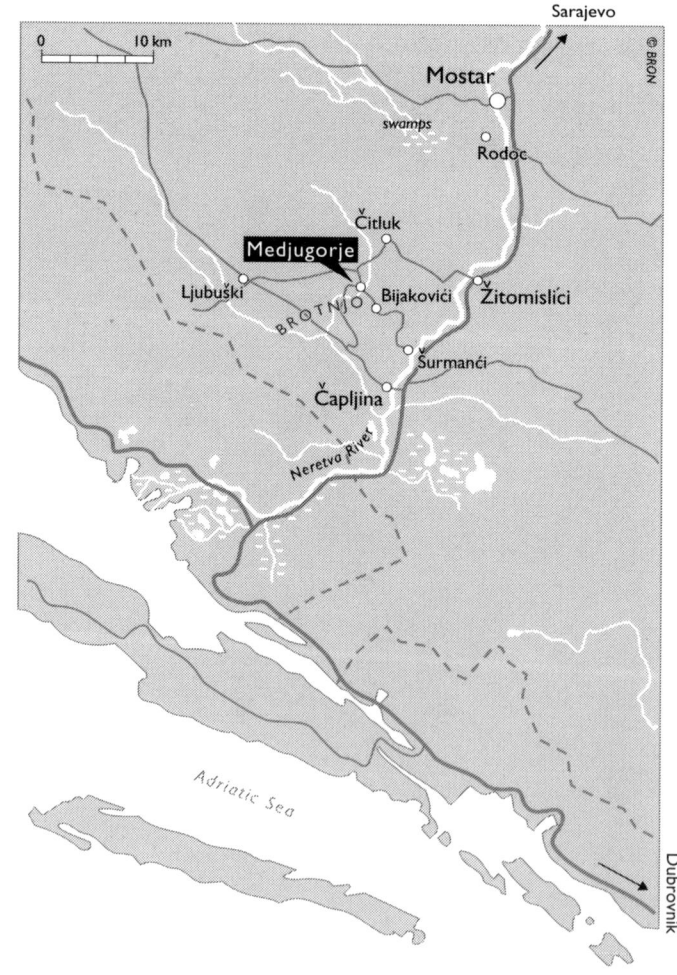

Chapter One

Introducing Medjugorje:
A Cook's Tour

'Mars must be more hospitable than western Herce-govina...' (Mischa Glenny 1992)

The plane circled Rodoc several times before it could land. Up until the outbreak of the war in 1991, in principle the former Yugoslavian civil airline *Jugoslovenski Aerotransport* (JAT) could use this military airfield south of Mostar. They just never knew whether they were going to get permission or not. The stories have it that if the tour operator of a chartered plane was not willing to pay the *surtaks*, a 'variable' tax the local military commander could levy at will, there was no way to land. The passengers, without exception pilgrims, would simply be informed that the weather at Rodoc was too rough.[1] In cases like this, the flight plan had to be altered and the plane rerouted to the civil airports at Split or Dubrovnik. For the pilgrims, this implied an extra half-day of travelling by touring car through rugged mountain territory. Ever since the war, this has been the route for all pilgrims because heavy bombing put Rodoc 'out of order'.

If everything went according to plan, the passengers would disembark at a small airport in a valley surrounded by mountains, just like most of the towns in Bosnia Hercegovina. Luggage retrieval and customs formal-ities were extremely time-consuming, and the suspicious attitude of the military personnel often sent chills up the pilgrims' spines.

To release some of the tension, a heavy-set Dutch lady sang the first notes of a religious song her group had practised in the plane under the leadership of the Franciscan priest accompanying them. A soldier roughly tugged the poor lady out of the line and shouted at her at length in Serbo-

1

Croat. It was not until the Franciscan priest apologized in Italian to a military officer that the incident was settled. (We were later told that the personnel at Rodoc consisted almost entirely of Serb soldiers who were definitely not happy with the events in Medjugorje, which were viewed in their circles as dangerous manifestations of Croat nationalism.)

Outside an old touring car was waiting to take the pilgrims to Medjugorje, a distance of thirty or forty kilometres. After a few kilometres the road, covered with a sturdy layer of tar, turned down into the valley of the Neretva River. This steep valley, cut deep into the mountainside by the turbulent river, has served as an important natural border for centuries (Malcolm 1994). It has also been a marker in the most recent war in Bosnia Hercegovina: on the eastern shore, high in the mountains, the Serb soldiers have taken their positions, and from there they can barrage and besiege large parts of the western region, where the Croats are dominant. Muslim enclaves are—or were—located on both sides of the magnificent river. On either side, the colours grey and white are dominant. The limestone formations, including sinks, ravines and underground streams, are barren and inhospitable. Only the riverside is touched with green, and some small-scale market gardens are visible. Here and there, clusters of little white houses are the closest thing to villages in this thinly populated area of southwestern Hercegovina.

About twenty kilometres further down the road, just past Žitomislići, the bus left the thoroughfare that goes to the Adriatic coast via Čapljina and Metkovic. Across the bridge, where vicious fighting had taken place, the driver shifted to a lower gear because the road was steep and filled with hairpin bends, some so sharp the bus could not manoeuvre them in one try. A few pilgrims were afraid, due to a fear of heights or because they felt the road would dissolve into thin air. The driver, however, was accustomed to all these emotions and with a few aptly chosen comments in German and a cheerful grin, he managed to break the tension. When the bus reached a pass carved near the top of the mountainside, it stopped for an hour's break. The driver said the bus 'needed a rest'. For a small price, the pilgrims could buy soft drinks he seemed to conjure up out of the blue. Out of nowhere, a few women (relatives of his?) appeared and began to spread out a quilt. With a great deal of care and somewhat theatrical gestures, they put an assortment of devotional objects and other knick-knacks on display. This immediately set the pilgrims in motion, and with no traces of fear or fatigue they purchased virtually every item the women had to sell.

The pass gave access to the Brotnjo, a plateau measuring approximately ten by twenty kilometres and surrounded by mountains. A small portion of the plateau is extremely fertile; grapes and tobacco are grown there for the market, and vegetables and fruit for the peasants' own consumption. The famous *Žilavka* and *Blatina* come from this area: these wines were popular at the Austrian royal court and in the administrative centres of the Ottoman Empire.

Most of the Brotnjo is stony, and good arable land for crop-growing is rare. For centuries, men from these parts have had to abandon their homes and go elsewhere to try and earn a living. Since the 1960s, many of them have gone as *Gastarbeiter* (migrant workers) to Austria, former West Germany, Belgium, Sweden and Switzerland, leaving their wives and children to see to the tobacco and vineyards, the cows and the sheep. It is they who now pit their wits against alternating floods and draught and the unyielding rocky soil. When the men return, they bring the late twentieth century with them. As a result, a curious mixture of modernity and back-wardness characterizes life on the Brotnjo.

After an hour of cooling off, the bus hit the road again, a road that is narrow, winding, and full of potholes. After a few kilometres, Čitluk came into sight. It is an unimpressive town with a population of approxi-mately 4,000 that serves as administrative centre for most of the Brotnjo, with the rest served by the town of Ljubuški to the south.

A few kilometres further, after another small pass, the priest an-nounced we were approaching Medjugorje. The pilgrims started sponta-neously singing and praying when the Virgin Mary's most recent shrine came into view.

The first impression was one of chaos. The houses, old and new, com-pleted and half-finished, seemed to have been dropped here and there alongside a road in the process of being paved. Ten years earlier there were hardly any houses here and the road was little more than a cart track, never more than three metres wide, with sheep, hens, goats, don-keys and small mountain cows wandering about. Ever since, construction has been going on at a feverish pace to house the pilgrims and cope with the traffic. It is as if everyone invests the money earned as *Gastarbeiter* or by giving pilgrims bed and board as quickly as possible in the houses.

Virtually all the villagers were engaged in construction of one kind or another, the men carrying stones, bags of cement, lengths of pipe for the water supply; the women and children shovelling the sand and stones that had been dropped beside the road into wheelbarrows and moving them slowly toward their farmyards as the elderly hauled boards and roof tiles.

3

A rotund pilgrim barely escaped being knocked to the ground by a bundle of swishing plastic pipes the owner was hastily transporting to his yard.

When the road curved at the rickety bridge over the Lukoc River, the ugly twin-towered church built of breeze blocks and concrete slabs came into view. On either side of the steadily expanded road to the church were souvenir shops, cafes and tiny restaurants. Less than five years ago, piles of rubbish left behind by residents, tourists and wandering goats dominated the scene. For many of the pilgrims, the colossal church of St James—much too large for its own parish, but in Hercegovina nothing is too large for God's house—is the sacred centre. Here masses are held in at least six languages, hour after hour, day after day.

The yard around the church has been altered and expanded every year, because like everyone else, the local clergymen are oriented toward the future. On a large lawn to the left of the entrance, dozens of Franciscans until recently would hear the confessions of the faithful, who waited patiently in long lines. Nowadays the confession area has been expanded and equipped with more than forty wooden confessional booths. Priests and pilgrims alike say they much prefer the open-air confessions, because in summer, when the pilgrimage is in full swing, it is hard to breathe in the stuffy little booths. The bishop, however, has prescribed the booths.

Behind the church, there is a sort of annex, a mainly open structure where younger people are often received. In front of the church is a huge square with benches and trees where tired pilgrims can rest, eat, or write postcards. In the 'good old days' before the war, when pilgrims were still coming to Medjugorje from around the globe, the square, or at any rate the open part of it, used to be packed with pilgrims who couldn't get into the crowded church. They would listen to the mass on the public address system of loudspeakers fastened to the church. Since the war, the area around the church has been virtually deserted, and the immense proportions of the open space are clearly visible.

Pilgrims sometimes compare the part of the square that is lined with benches to purgatory: you come in easily, but once there you are stung almost non-stop by bees attracted to the scents of soft drinks, deodorant and after-shave. The doctor who gives first aid in an annex of the parish house speaks of an unstoppable calamity.

To the right of the church is a large empty lot where Caritas (an international Roman Catholic relief organization) set up tents in 1993 to give refugees food, shelter and clothing. Medjugorje is now home to quite a few refugees. Since 1994, UNPROFOR has also been using the lot as storage space.

The parish house is across from the church. It is a large, roomy building that has been enlarged almost every year. This is where the Franciscan priests live who administer the parish and the devotion. Before the apparitions, usually three to five priests lived here, and they were responsible for the spiritual care of the vast parish. Since the apparitions began, their ranks have steadily increased, and nowadays about twenty clergymen live there. The parish house has a spacious bomb-proof cellar where services can be held if circumstances call for it. A small room should also be mentioned where for several years the seers would receive their apparitions. The premises also have a wing housing several Franciscan nuns, who are in charge of the housekeeping and other duties.

Just before the war, the Franciscans built a separate guest house on their property, mainly meant for their colleagues from abroad who came to assist them in the busy season. In short, the priests of the Franciscan order are amply and well represented in the devotion centre of Medjugorje.

At the spot where a little church once stood, a meditation garden with a chapel was recently opened. Only a few years ago, there was a barely paved circuit here with traffic jams worse than in many European metropolises. Buses, taxis, lorries and private cars were all trying to get wherever it was they were going, beeping their horns so loudly it disturbed the services at the church. Nowadays, it is easier for traffic to detour around it. To the left, there is the byway to Mount Šipovac, now referred to as Križevac or Mountain of the Cross, a shrine visited every day by numerous pilgrims. To the right, a narrow road leads to Bijakovići, the tiny village where the seers live and the site of Podbrdo, the mountain where the seers say they received their first messages from the Virgin Mary. Podbrdo, referred to by almost all the pilgrims as Apparition Hill, attracts hordes of pilgrims every day. Every year the steep path alongside the mountain becomes more crowded with little tents that are eventually replaced by more permanent structures.

The construction fever has affected day-to-day life in Bijakovići as well. Almost all the people of the hamlet consisting of one long street are adding rooms to their homes in an effort to get their share of the 'tourist gold'. Nowadays almost all the houses there have a few extra rooms and a dining room for guests. A few villagers, quick to recognize the new source of income, have built two or even three houses for themselves. In addition, some enterprising families have little grocery stores attached to their houses, where the pilgrims can buy food, soda, ice cream, soap and a variety of other merchandise. Other locals have built an—often not yet completed—room attached to their houses where they sell devotional articles that have been blessed by the seers, since that makes them worth more. The local clergymen are not happy with these developments. According to the shopkeepers, it is simply because the church has its own sales point, which until recently was under a garage at the side of the church. Other villagers have turned parts of their homes into cafeterias. There pilgrims can listen to blaring pop music or Croat torch songs while enjoying their soft drinks, Turkish coffee, hamburgers and sandwiches. In their improvised shop, two enterprising young men from Bijakovići sell video tapes showing various religious events at the Peace Centre. One of them recently started making videotapes on the spot to meet with whatever wishes the pilgrims might have. The local population has also started to be more interested in having weddings and other festivities recorded. And in the summer of 1994 I even noticed one of the two entrepreneurs videotaping a funeral at the churchyard in Bijakovići; a member of the family had asked him to do so.

Some of the houses look strikingly modern, with double-glazed tinted window panes, solar energy panels on the roof, spacious garages and a nice parking spot out in front. The houses of the seers do not look especially renovated, although their relatives' homes are certainly large and modern.

What is also noticeably large and modern is the white complex at the end of Bijakovići, which was completed in mid-1994. It is a guest house with a nuns' residence hall and a chapel attached to it. This hyper-modern complex is the proud possession of two female congregations from Belgium and Italy. Together they opened the guest house, and eventually hope to turn it into an independent convent. Up to now, they have not been able to arrange many activities. The grapevine has it that local Franciscans and a small female congregation in the vicinity are obstructing them.

Medjugorje and Bijakovići constitute the core of a parish, which also includes the villages of Miletina, Vionica and Šurmanci. Medjugorje is the largest of the villages, and together with the second-largest, Bijakovići, it is the centre of the devotion. The other villages are considerably smaller, and with the exception of Šurmanci, they play little role in the devotion or in this book.

With approximately 1,300 inhabitants divided over 400 households, Medjugorje is twice as large as Bijakovići. The two villages are separated by a strip of fertile land about 1,000 metres wide and 3,000 metres long, divided into small plots. For centuries, this 'oasis' in the barren, rocky region has been a bone of contention, causing hostility between the two villages.

The valley is traversed by a number of small roads, cart tracks that used to only lead to the small vineyards and tobacco fields. Nowadays the pilgrims use them to get quickly from the church in Medjugorje to Apparition Hill and back again. With their white hats or caps to protect them from the bright sunshine and their light clothes, you see them walking back and forth all day, like ants in the grass, singing and praying. Italians make the most noise and are most apt to be carrying statues of saints. From a distance, you can easily make out the Americans and Canadians, who are often slow-moving and overweight. They say hello to everyone they meet, and pay a great deal of attention to every flower, plant and tree they see, which is usually 'marvellous,' 'gorgeous' or 'wonderful'. Germans and Austrians are generally subdued and more disciplined, often to the extent of being sombre. The Filipinos, who tend to visit Medjugorje in large numbers, are quiet, intense and rugged; even at the hottest part of the day, when everyone else seeks shelter in the shade, they happily set out for Apparition Hill or Križevac.

In recent years, more and more white spots have appeared in this 'green heart' of the devotion centre. Not surprisingly, they are tiny stalls or sheds where devotional items or snacks are sold. Indeed, the local population goes all out in every way to please the pilgrims.

About halfway between Medjugorje and Bijakovići, there is a noman's-land where nothing is grown or sold. That is where the people of the two towns keep a careful eye on each other.

Like a sheltering arch around the villages, a spur of the Trtla Mountains separates them from the rest of the southern Brotnjo plateau. The spectacular finishing point of the mountain range is the 1200-metre peak of Mount Križevac. From its top, there is a view of almost the entire Brotnjo. This awe-inspiring peak is officially within the borders of Medjugorje; the rest of the mountain range is in Bijakovići territory. The villagers have built their homes like a ribbon along the foothills above the fertile valley.

The feelings aroused by the steep mountainsides with sparse touches of green are highly ambivalent. It is a popular hunting region, but it is also the home of lethally poisonous snakes locally called *poskok* and *crno strik*, and wolves that attack the villages in the winter. This is where people come to hide from guerrillas, police, and blood feuds, but also where people come to 'settle accounts'. Precious water comes down from the mountains, but so do the dreaded hot fall winds and hailstorms that can destroy entire vineyards and tobacco crops. In short, the Trtla Mountains bring joy and danger alike, and have always appealed to the imagination.

Note to Chapter One

1. The poor weather conditions argument was not completely unfounded. The vicinity of Mostar is known as a region of changeable weather where violent storms develop quickly.

Chapter Two

The Blessed Virgin Appears: Genesis and Evolution of a Devotional Regime

'The church is as much a political actor as the state ... because it is itself a body subject to internal ... rivalry and the struggle over resources and policies.' (Pedro Ramet 1985b)

It was on the 24th of June, 1981, that *Gospa*, as the Blessed Virgin is locally called, allegedly appeared before six children who were playing on Podbrdo, just outside Bijakovići. Since then, apparitions reportedly have taken place almost daily, right up to this very day, and they have attracted an impressive number of pilgrims from inside and outside ex-Yugoslavia.

From the very start, Medjugorje has been a controversial devotion. The bishop of Mostar, whose jurisdiction includes the parish of Medjugorje, and his diocesan priests are bitter opponents. They forbid worshippers to make pilgrimages to Medjugorje or otherwise take part in the 'theatrical practices'. In other respects as well, they do not refrain from sabotaging the devotion, which they continually characterize as 'misleading' and 'untruthful'. On the other hand, local Franciscan friars, priests who are entrusted with the pastoral care of the parish of Medjugorje, stimulate and support this 'special grace'. They view the conduct of the bishop and his priests as 'debasing for God and the people' and they accuse these opponents of 'lovelessness' and 'the desire for usurpation'. The secular authorities (until 1989 Communists) are just as involved. Initially, they used severely repressive measures; later, their policies were more relaxed. Rome has made no official statement about the devotion, but has adopted a wait-and-see attitude for the time being.

Why do the apparitions continue for such an unprecedentedly long time? Why is there antagonism between officials of the same church? Why does Rome make no official statement? Why does the devotion nevertheless attract enormous numbers of worshippers? These are just a few of the many questions that emerge.

Apparitions and pilgrimages have frequently been described in terms of rivalry, tension, and protest within a community of the faithful; less attention has been paid to religious elites and their roles in these manifestations of 'popular religion' (e.g. Campbell 1982; Christian 1973, 1984; Tentori 1982; Turner and Turner 1978).

In this chapter I will argue that the Medjugorje devotion is a function of changing power relations between two categories of religious elites in the area, the diocesan priests and the Franciscan friars.[1]

Background

Franciscan Hegemony (1370-1960)

Until the beginning of the 1960s, the Franciscan friars reigned supreme in the pastoral care of most of the diocese of Mostar. According to Rome, it has always been the intention that these missionaries, after building up the parochial infrastructure, would make room for a diocesan establishment to be formed by a bishop appointed by Rome and secular clergy designated by him. Since their arrival in the region (around 1370), however, the Franciscans have interpreted their assignment differently.[2] With the help of one of the last independent Bosnian kings, they not only managed to drive out the *Bogumils* Rome viewed as heretics; they also managed to firmly establish their own regime (Fine 1975; Mandić 1978).[3] The long-standing domination of Bosnia and Hercegovina by the Ottoman Turks (1463-1878) was not unfavourable in this respect. In return for considerable amounts of protection money, the Ottoman rulers granted the Franciscans exclusive jurisdiction over Catholics in the area. The Turkish domination also implied that the Franciscan friars remained safe from control by Rome—the Turks' archenemy—and could expand and consolidate their influence in spiritual and material respects (Fine 1975; Gavranović 1935).

The Franciscan hegemony seemed to come to an end when in 1878 what is today Bosnia Hercegovina fell under the authority of the Austro-Hungarian Empire. The Habsburg ruler worked together with Rome to produce a diocesan division for the area and a parochial subdivision, after which its bishops and secular priests were appointed.[4] Mostar also fell under this regulation. But partly through massive pressure from the Franciscans on the Holy See, the fathers managed to maintain their power in this predominantly Catholic area which had been one of their most secure strongholds. Along with their own provincial Father Superior, they did have to accept an 'outside' bishop as leader. An agreement was made with this prelate which was later (in 1923) ratified by Rome. In the terms of this agreement, the Franciscans kept the majority of the parishes and could claim as theirs all the parishes they would build up through missionary work among Muslims and members of the Serbian Orthodox Church.[5] In return, the Franciscan priests would contribute to a diocesan seminary and help recruit seminarians. The first part of this agreement has been observed by the Franciscans. However, partly as a result of their own well-organized recruitment networks, they were able to keep the number of diocesan seminarians very low. This repeatedly led to friction between the two categories of specialists, Franciscan and diocesan (Quaestio 1979; Gavranović 1935).

In the decades that followed, the Franciscans managed to set up nine new parishes, so that they controlled sixty-three of the total of seventy-nine parishes. In addition, their regime in that area included twenty-nine monasteries, five seminaries, a few hospitals, various business establishments, and considerable land holdings (Ilić 1974). In short, at the beginning of the 1940s the religious arena of the diocese of Mostar was characterized by a firmly established Franciscan regime and a weakly developed diocesan regime.

World War II, and even more the establishment of the communist state which followed, brought about great changes. A series of legal measures, partly intended to nationalize the Roman Catholic Church in what was then Yugoslavia, hit the dominant regime the hardest. Franciscans thus lost nearly all their property and authority: their private schools, their nursing homes, hospitals, and other health-care institutions. Only the parishes remained. Since there were harsh sentences for missionary activities, this power base could not be enlarged. In spite of the great losses, the Franciscans still managed to maintain their supremacy for some time. This was partially possible because, in contrast to the opponent, they still had at their disposal sufficient religious specialists to continue parochial pastoral care.[6] But the days of Franciscan hegemony appeared to be numbered.

Diocesanization (1960-1979)

At the beginning of the 1960s, relations between church and state became less strained. Each party seemed to realize that some acceptance of the other was a requirement for its own survival and development. Diplomatic relations were renewed during Vatican II, and in 1966 Rome and the Yugoslav government signed an agreement in which mutual rights and obligations were established.[7]

For the bishop of Mostar, these developments made it possible to extend the diocesan regime. Unlike his colleagues, this prelate had already clearly spoken out in favour of the state government. He had even argued that Christianity and Marxism went together very well (Ramet 1985; Rynne 1965). Indeed, he was one of the first bishops of the country to state openly that he recognized the priests' associations founded and controlled by the state, and he even encouraged his priests to join.[8] This strategy's advantages were soon apparent. In 1966, the bishop signed an agreement in secret—though it quickly became a public secret—with the authorities of Bosnia Hercegovina. The latter guaranteed facilities and educational grants for priests in exchange for a degree of state control over the selection of seminarians and appointment of parish priests. In the meantime, the prelate was also active on another front: in Rome. In 1965, he was able to have the 1923 agreement concerning parochial property revised. In this revision, twenty-one of the sixty-three Franciscan parishes came under the bishop's jurisdiction; with respect to the remaining forty-two, according to Rome, the parties—the bishop and the Franciscans—were to consult with each other and harmoniously reach a solution. Two years later, in 1967, after futile discussions with the Franciscans and through mediation by the Holy See, the bishop managed to bring another twelve parishes under his control, so that the Franciscans' domain shrank to thirty parishes (Quaestio 1979). In doing so, the Mostar prelate won the sympathy of the state-minded Catholic small-town bourgeoisie, but at the same time brought upon himself the hatred of the nationalistic and anti-state peasantry from many small villages.[9]

In the years that followed, the transfer of the parishes to the diocesan priests did not proceed flawlessly. Most of the new priests had just completed their studies and came from well-to-do urban backgrounds. Many of the faithful viewed them as an extension of the state, which was still hardly friendly toward religion.[10] In many of the parishes there was open resistance to this diocesanization. The parishioners, not infrequently covertly helped by the Franciscans, refused to open the church doors to the new priests, who, sometimes after a stiff beating, had to leave defeated. In a few cases, diocesan priests and Franciscans even publicly came to blows, with the populace cheering them on (Ramet 1985). It was only after police intervention that the diocesan priests could take possession of their new domain.

The tension and antagonism reached a peak in 1975, when Rome considered granting another five parishes to the bishop of Mostar. For the Franciscans, these were precisely the parishes they could not do without, as since ancient times they had been their most important area for recruiting personnel (Quaestio 1979). The priests were prepared to go to any extremes to maintain these 'lifelines'. In an open letter they accused the bishop of a deliberate isolation policy. In addition, the Franciscan Father Superior sent a letter (evidently worded in no uncertain terms) to Rome, explaining the precarious situation of his fellow brothers and pointing out that the plans were contrary to previous agreements. The result was that the Father Superior was suspended. The bishop of Mostar interpreted this as an excommunication and pronounced the presence of all Franciscans in the parishes to be in conflict with church law. Legally, or so the prelate thought, the parishes had thus come under his command. Although the bishop was in no hurry to take over—he was probably under pressure from the secular authorities, who wanted an orderly turnover—the Franciscans were still in dire straits. They had nowhere to turn. There were no other forms of pastoral care they could engage in, such as education or health care, and there were heavy sentences for missionary work among non-believers. A number of Franciscans emigrated to Western Europe, where they found pastoral work in the numerous communities of Croat workers and political exiles. But 'God's salvation was at hand', said one older Franciscan emphatically during an interview.

Genesis and Development

'Mystical Preparations' (1979-1981)

Information about the events that followed—in Franciscan circles referred to as 'mystical preparations'—is difficult to uncover and surely not complete. In 1979, Father Branko, who had served in the parish of Medjugorje for years, attended a meeting of the Charismatic Renewal

Movement at a monastery in Italy.[11] After expressing his great concern about the developments in the diocese of Mostar (according to widespread claims in Franciscan circles), he received two prophesies from some of the leading figures of the movement. In one of them the priest was seen in the midst of a fast-growing multitude, and from where he sat, there flowed streams of living water. The other read: 'Do not worry; I shall send you My Mother and everyone shall listen to Her'.

Shortly afterwards, according to Franciscan circles, Father Branko was told to return to his old parish of Medjugorje and make preparations to be dictated to him. Once he was home again, he began to teach the Franciscan regimen for the laity in a catechism class for children. Prayers, fasting, confession, atonement, and the recitation of the rosary all played an important role in it. Some time later, a similar class was formed for the women of the parish. Father Branko told the women and children about the 'special grace' God would reveal to the children of Medjugorje. It was intended for everyone and they had to pray for its hastening. Draga Bosanković, an aged widow who lives quite near some of the seers, vividly remembers those days. Draga recalled:

'There was something extraordinary in the air ... like spring, but much stronger. ... We all felt it ... all the women up here. ... We had our rosary when we went to class at the rectory, but we kept it with us day and night. We were so busy imagining what was going to happen that we forgot about our work ... The men were joking and shouting at us. Some of them thought we used drugs and things. We neglected the fireplace, the cooking, the goats ... But, mind, they also had a feeling that something special was going to happen'.

In 1980, two village children fell seriously ill. When recovery through medical means no longer seemed possible, the children's mothers sought the help of Father Branko. From the children's catechism class, he formed prayer groups to pray and keep vigil over the sick children. On the 8th of September (the day of Mary's birth), after a few weeks of intensive prayer, recovery set in. Out of gratitude, all the persons concerned, along with a number of other parishioners, journeyed to the famous shrine of Marija Bistrica. A special devotion for the Virgin Mary was set up in Medjugorje.

In the early spring of 1981, according to Father Leonard, the second pastor of the parish, 'special grace revealed itself once again to the children'. Separately and in different places, six young people from the catechism class each found old and costly Franciscan rosaries. After inquiries in the village revealed they did not belong to anyone, the children went

14

to Father Branko. The clergyman was joyful. 'These were clear signs of their selection by God and His coming grace', he recalled in an interview. Father Branko urged those young people to pray fervently every day with each other, with him, and also with the women.

'Our Lady Appears' (1981)

On June 24, 1981, the moment seemed to have arrived. Many local informants remember that it was a sultry summer evening, characteristic of the area at that time of the year. After evening mass, six young people played and romped about on their way home. On Podbrdo, not far from the tobacco fields at the edge of Bijakovići, they suddenly saw a luminous figure. Curious, but also somewhat apprehensive, they ran toward it. It was *Gospa*, they immediately knew, who smilingly beckoned them closer. After a few heartening remarks and a promise to return the next evening, the figure vanished. The youngsters hastened back to the rectory, where they gave an account of what had happened to Father Vjekoslav (Father Branko had just left for Mostar).

Within hours the whole village knew about it. Accompanied by a rapidly growing crowd of villagers and people from the neighbouring hamlets, the seers went back to the hill the following evening. The Madonna, who was said to be seen and heard only by the young visionaries, gave messages to pass on to everyone. Peace and forbearance among God's people, the priests, and all the people of the world. These have been the continually recurring themes of the messages up to the present day. In addition, it is claimed that the Madonna gave and continues to give very concrete instructions and assignments. They are meant for an ever-changing variety of people, but peace and forbearance are nearly always part of them (cf. Blais 1985).[12] From the outset the Madonna, who wants to be called the Queen of Peace, urged people to pray, fast, confess, and take communion. The Mother of God reportedly has also entrusted the young seers with ten secrets. In due course, they are to be revealed to all people to enable them to believe in God's love and almighty power.

In peasant societies, unusual news travels fast. Consequently, the number of participants at the meetings every evening on Podbrdo soon had grown to a few thousand. Many reportedly received special forms of grace such as recovery from illness, and numerous persons beheld spectacular light phenomena. With much the same speed, the relatively new devotional movement became entangled in conflicts, first with the civil authorities and later with the diocese and Rome.

Conflicts, Confrontations, and Expansion (1981-1990)

The miraculous news spread like wildfire through the rough countryside of Hercegovina. In no time it had reached Čitluk, the district capital. The local police took immediate measures against this disturbance of the peace and closed access to the mountain where the apparitions took place. The six seers were subjected to a thorough investigation. In the communist press, the devotion was the subject of exhaustive attention. It was continually depicted as a 'fascist' movement which constituted a threat to the unity of the Yugoslav people (Cviić 1982). Church life, the religious leaders, and the faithful also had regularly to bear the brunt of criticism. The sounding of the church bell was prohibited. (It was thought to be 'provocative'.) The church building and the rectory were searched on several occasions for 'propaganda literature hostile to the state'. Sermons in the church were frequently disturbed by the noise of low-circling helicopters from the police and army. Money from the church collection was confiscated a number of times. Party activists monitored church services daily for 'imperialist propaganda'. The local priests had to appear twice a week at the police station in Čitluk. Worshippers were repeatedly apprehended and, without any form of trial, locked up for days at the district prison (Ramet 1985a).

Jozo Marković (32), a local mechanic and a relative of one of the seers, became excited again when discussing the actions of the militia in the early days of the movement. In 1989 he recalled: 'First we were interrogated, beaten, and locked up. But now that those bastards see that there is money in it, they come on a Sunday morning and rub shoulders with the locals to buy their land ... They want it for building ... lucrative pensions, hostels and things ... When I helped the old folks up the Podbrdo they caught me and they took me to their boss in Čitluk. It was a terrible time ... I lost my job in a garage in Čitluk. My father ... he lives not far from here ... they took his old age pension. My brother was a customs officer ... He was recovering from an operation ... they said it was cancer ... One day, he got a letter stating that he was fired because of his involvement in the production of anti-state propaganda ... And look at those bastards now! I told you, they smell money ... They try to steal it from the people and the priests ... wherever they can...' Cursing, he concluded: 'One day, we'll fight them. We'll strike back!'

All the overt forms of intimidation, however, failed to lead to the results desired by the authorities. Soon after the mountain was made off-limits, the apparitions started again, but at a different spot: before evening mass in one of the side rooms of the church. The campaign pursued in the communist press also failed to have the desired result. On the contrary, it helped publicize the unusual events in Medjugorje so that ever larger numbers of people made pilgrimages. In short, it was partly due to the repressive actions of the authorities that the devotional movement expanded.

After some two years, the authorities became more accommodating. The mountain was reopened and the grounds near the church were made available for the devotion. Every day, about forty Franciscans heard confessions of an ever-growing mass of pilgrims, some from abroad. The official explanation for the greater lenience was that church leaders in the area had adhered to the policies of the authorities. Another reason, perhaps of equal importance, was of a financial nature: the pilgrims—especially those from abroad—brought a lot of money into the local economy.[13] Furthermore, the spiritual leaders in Medjugorje allegedly paid considerable annual 'taxes' to the local authorities.[14]

Even though the authorities and the Franciscans seemed to have moved somewhat closer to each other, the conflicts between the latter and the bishop of Mostar and his diocesan priests went on virtually unabated. But the antagonism also unintentionally contributed to the expansion of the devotional regime. Almost from the beginning, the diocese must have viewed the apparitions and their 'guidance' by the Franciscans as a threat.[15] After the bishop, in a private discussion, unsuccessfully demanded silence from the Franciscans of Medjugorje, he switched to a tactic of open confrontation. In accordance with church law, he set up a committee to investigate the authenticity of the apparitions. When this committee proved unable to detect any inconsistencies with ecclesiastical teachings, the bishop dissolved it and appointed a second one.

When this committee failed to reach a clear verdict, the prelate again redirected his efforts. He presented the events in Medjugorje for discussion at the Yugoslav Bishops' Conference. This conference issued a communique, which was read aloud from the pulpit in all parishes, announcing that the bishops collectively were against 'official' (church-organized) pilgrimages to the site; unofficial journeys by individuals and groups were not forbidden.[16] The bishop of Mostar must have interpreted this as support for his own policies. In a pastoral letter (which was ignored in the Franciscan parishes), he prohibited worshippers in his diocese from making pilgrimages to Medjugorje. Offenders would be barred from receiving the sacraments.[17] This tactic, however, did not hit its intended target, but had the opposite effect. The number of worshippers from the diocese who regularly went on pilgrimage to Medjugorje was already very large. Many of these were now in fact forced to go to Medjugorje, to receive the sacraments in one of the Franciscan parishes. Consequently, the size of these religious communities grew with unprecedented speed. For the Franciscans this was reason to ask their order's Superior General in Rome for more parish personnel. The Holy See must have granted this request, for since the end of 1984 the number of Franciscan priests working in the diocese of Mostar has risen from eighty to more than 120 (in 1989).

The diocese allegedly approached its opponent in a still stronger way. Through all sorts of contacts the Mostar 'headquarters' had the backgrounds of Franciscan priests investigated. Not infrequently they or their relatives were said to be or have been involved in nationalistic movements operating from bases inside and outside the country. By making this information public (in pamphlets, for example), the diocese in fact incited the arrest of Franciscan priests.[18] However, these confrontations also turned out to be to the advantage of the devotional movement. Nationalism in the countryside increased and became more closely interwoven with the movement. More Franciscans were considered political martyrs, which considerably enhanced their appeal.

After these direct confrontations, which had all unintentionally helped expand the devotion, the bishop of Mostar and his priests began to approach their opponents differently. Since 1985 or so, the diocesan strategy seems to have been completely directed to canon law. Through informants who have been continually present at the site, the diocese has had the devotion, the visionaries, the heavenly messages, and the officiating Franciscan friars carefully monitored, and everything that even hints at divergence from church teachings or tradition is reported to Rome. The Franciscans, however, hardly seem concerned about this surveillance. 'Rome now has another ear in Medjugorje', one friar noted ironically.

Franciscan Strategies and Tactics

The description so far might give the impression that the Franciscans have pursued a passive strategy, observing how the mechanism of 'victimization' works to their advantage. This impression is incorrect. Ever since the first apparitions, they have been active on different fronts to strengthen their position in the area of Mostar. From the beginning, the devotion has been directed toward achieving international support and recognition. The Franciscan supervisors did not wait for the opinion of the episcopal investigation committee, but invited experts from the international apparition network to give their opinion (see for example, Laurentin 1984, 1985, 1986). In addition, the Franciscan Family is involved. This worldwide network of Franciscan friars and sisters and their lay following organizes pilgrimages to Medjugorje from a number of countries. Until recently the coordination took place in Steubenville, Ohio (USA), at the Franciscan centre, which was also in charge of the major lines of publicity policy about Medjugorje.[19] And, of course, the Franciscan-run Croat communities in Western Europe have also been mobilized. They help disseminate the 'heavenly messages' from Medjugorje, they organize pilgrimages to the site, and they financially support the education of young men from the area to become Franciscan priests. The devotional movement has also assured itself of international support and recognition in the (para)medical field. Medical specialists from Italy, Germany, France, and the United States are studying the registered cases of miraculous healing in Medjugorje. The (positive) results are widely published by Franciscan sources (Ramet 1985a).

On the home front, in the diocese of Mostar, an active strategy also has been pursued from the very beginning to stigmatize and deadlock the diocesan opponents and to incorporate as many laypersons as possible into the devotional movement. Through the visionaries, the bishop and his diocesan priests are reported to have received numerous messages and instructions from the Virgin Mary. One of the first messages was for the bishop of Mostar, stating that the prelate had wrongfully excommunicated a number of Franciscans. She encouraged the bishop to undertake a 'public reconciliation' with these 'sons of the church'. The diocesan priests also have been urged along this 'heavenly' course toward reconciliation.[20] The numerous messages and instructions did not remain secret for long. It became widely known that the Madonna reprimanded the bishop and his priests and supported their adversaries. (Local jokers may explain to the visitor that this is one of the major reasons why the infant Jesus has been crying so much lately. Others retort that there is another reason: Jesus cries because he has been missing his mother now for more than ten years.) This open stigmatizing has turned into an institution of sorts. On the Podbrdo and in the church, weekly 'intentions' have been prayed for the bishop and his priests, who are referred to by name. According to the seers, *Gospa* has urgently requested these prayers.

The effects of these tactical manoeuvres on the bishop and his priests are clear enough. They can no longer openly classify the messages and apparitions as untruths, because they would only further damage their position in the eyes of the faithful. A denunciation on the basis of canon law is also not possible, since Rome and the investigative committee have not yet made any definite pronouncements. On the other hand, recognition of the apparitions and messages is likewise out of the question. Then the bishop and his priests would play into the hands of their Franciscan adversaries. In short, the diocese is in a deadlock.

This impasse has given the Franciscans the opportunity once again to serve their former clientele. In this respect the seers and their 'heavenly' messages also play an important role. Through the children, the Madonna allegedly has informed a number of influential laypersons from the former Franciscan parishes that, together with their families and fellow villagers, they are to form prayer groups and meet regularly to pray for sick and needy neighbours. 'God will send His spirit to His children' is the message from Our Lady. In addition, for the dissemination of her message, the Virgin has made use of the miraculous ways people in Medjugorje are healed and converted. Our Lady has called upon the worshippers in the diocese to join in celebration at the site of her apparitions.

Lastly, the devotional movement has also pursued more than a passive strategy toward the Holy See. Along with a steady flow of diplomatic traffic between Medjugorje and Rome, which is almost completely kept from public view, as of mid-1986 three 'heavenly' messages have been issued from the sacral centre of Medjugorje to the Pope, and have been widely circulated in printed form. In the first message (1981), the Virgin Mary announced that she loves the Pope and protects him during his travels. In the second (1982), Our Lady said she cherishes the Holy Father and encourages him in his efforts for peace. The third (1983) emphasized the urgent nature of Mary's announcements. Although there has been no formal reaction from Rome, one can speculate that it is hard to imagine these messages and their widespread publication having had no influence upon the position of the Holy See.

What began with six young people's supernatural experience in a small peasant village has developed into a firmly established Franciscan-run devotional regime with an impressive number of international branches. In the geographical centre of the movement, Medjugorje, this was evident up to 1991, one year before the war broke out in Bosnia Hercegovina. Every day pilgrims came from inside the country and abroad. Partly due to the large numbers, the formerly spontaneous collective manifestations of faith had made way for more routine daily practices according to a fixed schedule. The pilgrims first visited the mountain of the apparitions which, since so many of them take a stone as a souvenir, has come to look more and more like a crater. Next, they were led to a field adjacent to the church, where several dozen Franciscans heard confessions. Afterwards, the faithful took communion at the church. There was also an opportunity to visit the seers (at least two of them were always present) and ask them to intercede with Our Lady or receive their prayers with the laying-on of hands. (People who had been cured or had received some other answer to their prayers were requested to record the fact at the rectory. During the summer months, between 200 and 500 statements were made daily.) Then the pilgrims could talk to people in the village and the neighbouring hamlets who had been healed or received other forms of special grace. About six o'clock in the evening was the climax: in a small room in the rectory, only accessible to priests, Our Lady appeared to the seers for a few minutes. Her messages for the faithful were usually announced by a Franciscan priest. This was done over a public address system, so the numerous persons in the church and on the adjacent field could hear them. (All the messages were recorded on tape by the Franciscans, and many pilgrims used portable recorders to tape the heavenly messages, which were translated into several languages.) Then the seers went outside, and, as cameras buzzed and flashbulbs went off, they hurried to the church building. On their way they were repeatedly touched by waiting pilgrims hoping for some of the supernatural power believed to be present in the young people. In the church a mass was celebrated, usually by a dozen Franciscans and a large number of guest-priests from all over the world. For the rest of the evening, the worshippers could visit with the seers again to hear whether Our Lady had given a special message for them, or to have them bless objects brought from home and devotional objects purchased at the site. On warm summer nights one could hear singing and subdued

subdued conversation until the next morning. Then the same schedule began again for a new group of pilgrims. (The foreigners among them had already spent a few days visiting other sights 'advised' by the state authorities, so they arrived at the place of mercy somewhat lighter in the monetary sense.)

In addition to this routinization, a process of functional differentiation had taken place at the devotion centre. The tasks of the religious leaders had been considerably expanded. In 1990 a rotating staff of at least fifty Franciscan friars was present. The departments of finance, visitor registration, documentation and 'special pastoral care' alone were staffed by at least ten full-time Franciscan priests and a few Franciscan sisters who formerly attended to the local elementary school. In addition, a large number of faithful villagers were more or less professionally involved with the daily devotion. There were people who worked as guides or to preserve order, and others who told of their own miraculous healing. Villagers were employed to serve meals and refreshments or to offer pilgrims lodgings. Handymen and craftsmen manufactured devotional objects, which their wives and children sold. Technicians were also needed for the mass of electrical apparatuses which were part of the standard equipment of the visionaries, the priests, and the numerous pilgrims. In short, almost all the villagers were in one way or another involved in the devotion. 'Everyone is supported by Our Lady', remarked a local cynic.[21]

The impact of the devotion on the local population was also of a more spiritual nature. Every morning and evening one could see large numbers of men, women, and children in freshly-laundered clothing devoutly walking to the church building. According to the local priests, it had become a habit among many to attend mass at least once a day. Even the communal shepherd, formerly a notorious drunkard, was a daily visitor of the church. Many people loyally followed the instructions of the Madonna. They prayed and fasted frequently, they read regularly in their Bibles, and they took Holy Communion. At least once a week many locals waited in long rows in the open field near the church, where Franciscans heard confession. The Medjugorje landlady of this author neatly summed up what many people in the parish thought: 'Since *Gospa* came here for the first time, vendettas have stopped and families are reunited. We are all happy and well-off, and we try to be friendly and hospitable. That's also what Our Lady teaches us: we must be an example for the world'.

In addition to Marian instructions and priestly teachings, miraculous healings had greatly contributed to the religious revival among the inhabitants of Medjugorje. Up to 1991, more than sixteen locals were said to have been cured of serious diseases as a result of the intercession of the Virgin Mary. Janko Sirola, 21, is a telling example. Good-looking and active in the local football club, he was highly popular among the boys and girls. Janko recounted: 'I had just passed my exam at the technical school in Mostar. When I came home for the summer to help my mother on the farm, I fell ill. The doctors said I would lose control over my legs, and I had a terrible pain in my back. It was a hopeless case. When the world seemed to tumble down on me, my mother and sister literally dragged me to the church. In the chapel we prayed and, thanks be to God, I felt the strength coming back into my legs. I can walk! I shouted. Later, my friends came to visit me. They were astounded. I asked them to accompany me to the church. Nowadays, some twenty of us help the Fathers with all sorts of things. And every day we are at mass. Some of us have decided to become priests'.

Referring to Janko and other miraculously cured persons in Medjugorje, Father Krsto joked: 'They are walking publicity. ... Morning, noon and night, day after day, the people up here see those witnesses of God's special grace. This is truly living faith'.

In many other parishes of the Mostar diocese a certain consolidation of the devotional movement had taken place. The more or less spontaneously formed prayer groups of the past had grown into imposing communities reminiscent of the religious brotherhoods of old. Spread throughout the diocese, there were in 1991 almost seventy such groups, each of which consisted of a number of families. The groups were called *Križari*, which literally means crusaders.[22] *Križari* had no status in canon law and had no formal leadership. The active nucleus almost always consists of a small group of laypersons who had been approached by the Virgin Mary in some special way.

A *Križari* group fulfilled a multitude of functions, locally for the members as well as for the movement in general. First and foremost, they continued as a prayer group. People gathered in the home or barn of one of the members three times a week, including once on Sunday, at the same time as mass is said in the parish churches controlled by the diocese. If possible, the Sunday meetings were attended by a Franciscan priest, who was then responsible for the Eucharist and other sacramental rites. Holding an alternative mass of this kind, however, was not without risks, since the law at the time forbade the practice of religion outside the state-recognized church buildings. The violation of this law had allegedly landed many Franciscans in jail—though they were quickly set free after paying ransom money. *Križari* groups also were mutual assistance organizations, with members supporting each other in the event of illness, accidents, death, and other calamities. The costs were covered by a fund, the majority of which came through the Franciscan friars from the devotional centre in Medjugorje. (This form of assistance has a recruiting effect.) *Križari* also served as reception centres for pilgrims who came from afar. Again, they were important junctions in a long-distance communication network. They received messages (heavenly and otherwise) from the centre and distributed them to the parishes. In the other direction, they saw to it that the centre received information about the local situation.[23] Last, these local branches of the movement acted as mobilization forces for pilgrimages to Medjugorje. Until the war, groups of worshippers continued to go there because it was generally believed that was where the 'power of mercy' was the greatest. People went there to have crosses and portraits of Our Lady blessed, to make confessions, and to receive the sacrament of the Eucharist. They went there to have their children baptized and to ask for recovery from illness, to take a vow or to give thanks for gifts received. In short, through a constant two-way flow of people and information, a Franciscan-run religious regime had (once again) taken shape in the diocese of Mostar.

Conclusions

In the preceding pages an attempt has been made to describe and explain the evolution of the Medjugorje devotional movement in terms of rivalry and competition between Franciscan priests and diocesan clergy. The promotion of the devotion by a threatened group of Franciscan friars turned out to be an effective defense strategy against diocesan expansionism. It goes without saying that not all apparitions and pilgrimages are the outcome of factionalism between order-clergy and diocesan priests. Indeed, there may be enough singularity about the Medjugorje case to suggest caution in claiming too much for the perspective adopted here. On the other hand, similar events in other countries under comparable circumstances seem to support the conclusion that Medjugorje is not unique. Order-priests in nineteenth-century Dutch Brabant (Bax 1987, 1992), and seventeenth-century New Spain (Oss 1978), seventeenth- and eighteenth-century Peru (Spier 1987), and seventeenth-century Eire (Corish 1985) are reported also to have taken recourse to stimulating apparitions in order to defend themselves against diocesan expansionism. Apparently, then, a relationship exists between (early?) diocese-formation and the occurrence of apparitions and devotions.

A few intriguing questions remain. First of all, why was the rivalry between the two religious elites so public and hostile? An important reason can undoubtedly be found in the specific configuration of which the religious leaders were part. It encompassed a secular as well as a church authority, both of which pursued an indistinct policy toward the two categories of religious elites. Whether intentionally or unintentionally, the two were thus set against one another. Since the two sorts of priests were both dependent upon the same (non-extendable) clientele for their livelihood, their competition had to be open.

A second question concerns the attitude of Rome. Why does the Holy See fail to make any official pronouncements about the apparitions? One can postulate that, at any rate for the time being, Rome has little choice. An official authorization presents certain problems. The results of the already stagnating diocesanization process achieved with such difficulty probably would not be helped at all. Diplomatic relations with the secular authorities would be damaged, and tensions between the two religious camps would only be increased. An official denial of the heavenly nature of the messages, however, is just as problematical. As yet, there do not appear to be any theological arguments for this position. In addition, the remarkable gains in new and re-activated worshippers would possibly be lost.

The spectacular growth constitutes another point of interest. In contrast to what is generally asserted about pilgrimages, the growth in this case has not been due to the standpoint of Rome but to the social strength of the religious elites connected to the devotion. What is concerned here is an extensive provincial order (the only one in the area) with a large amount of social cohesion (all of the members are in the same boat) and a strong historical tie to the local population who, for diverse forms of help, can appeal to a worldwide network of sympathizers. It is important to stress the crucial role of religious elites in the development of visionary movements. At approximately the same time as the first apparitions in Medjugorje, there was a report of a similar occurrence in another parish of the diocese. The Franciscans dissociated themselves from it, and the young devotion then died a peaceful death (Ramet 1985a, 1985b).

One last question is perhaps the most intriguing: Why have the apparitions continued for such an unusually long time and so regularly? A comparison with intra-religious power balances in other European societies can provide some clarification. Wherever the diocesan organization is firmly established, authorized devotional movements are coopted, their forms of worship are brought into agreement with the teachings of the church, and the seers are kept out of the public eye. This happens because they and their messages constitute a potential threat to the teachings of the church and the religious authorities (Christian 1973). The balance of power in the Mostar diocese would make it impossible to conceal the seers and their messages. The diocesan organization lacks the power to do so, and it is in the interest of the Franciscans to continue their presence. Outwardly the seers form an important defense: Rome, the bishop, and the priests of the diocese have limited leeway as a result. Inwardly the visionaries not only contribute to the maintenance of boundaries between the numerous 'basis organizations' and the diocesan-controlled parishes, but they also stimulate cohesion between the congregations, among themselves, and with the devotional centre. Thus, one might tend to postulate that the seers and their heavenly messages will disappear from the public view when, in the opinion of the Franciscans, some satisfactory solution has been found to the conflict that binds them to the bishop and his priests. This view, however, underestimates the power generated by the seers themselves and their influence on the (further) development of the devotional regime. This will be the focus of the next chapter.

Notes to Chapter Two

1. For the reader who is not familiar with the Roman Catholic Church, it is important to know that its leadership structure includes two types of religious specialists: the diocesan or secular clergy and the monastic or Order clergy. The diocesan clergy are supervised by their bishop. The monastic priests, members of religious Orders who usually live in monasteries, do not fall under the direct authority of diocesan bishops. In principle these two types of religious specialists have the same rights. They can hear confessions, say Mass, preside at baptisms and marriages, and administer the last sacraments to the dying. Thus diocesan and monastic priests are potential rivals, but more often than not, their rivalry remains latent. In addition to a widely propagated ethos of cooperation, this situation has to do with a specific division of labour. The primary task of the diocesan clergy is the administration of the parish and the spiritual care of the parishioners, whereas the monastic priests devote their energy to other sorts of work and to missionary work in particular. This division of labour affects how the

Church establishes itself in a new region. As a rule, Order priests are the first to settle in new territory. The primary task of these 'missionaries' is to set up an ecclesiastical infrastructure which includes parishes with chapels or churches and seminaries for the education of priests from the area. After some time, and with the approval of the secular authorities, Rome may go on to institute a diocesanization process for the area, including the transformation of the mission area into one or more dioceses and the replacement of the missionaries by priests from the diocese. Missionary processes often meet with severe problems, which have been relatively well-documented. Very little, however, is known about the intra-religious problems of diocese-formation.

2. In *Quaestio Hercegoviniensis* (1979) the Franciscan friars very emphatically stated that they do not see themselves as missionaries and that they were never considered as such by Rome. On the contrary, according to the discussion, Rome had entrusted the spiritual care of what is now the present diocese of Mostar-Duvno to the Franciscans in the fourteenth century. More information on the history of the Franciscans in the region can be found in: Fine 1975, 1987; Alexander 1979; Mandić 1978; Gavranović 1935; Guldeson 1964; Soldo 1964; Vego 1981; Rupčić 1937.

3. More information about Bogumils and Bogumilism is given in Chapter Six.

4. It goes without saying that Rome was in favour of such a form of management. For the Habsburg ruler, there was also the issue of marginalizing the Franciscans and, wherever possible, replacing them with loyal clergy. Well-organized and with strongly nationalistic sentiments, the Franciscans of Bosnia Hercegovina constituted too strong a centrifugal power, in the opinion of the ruler (cf. Alexander 1979; Gavranović 1935).

5. The Serbian Orthodox Church was established in 1204. It is one of the group of Orthodox Eastern Churches, the origin of which dates back to the Schism of 1054, which resulted in a division of the Byzantine Empire into an Eastern Empire and a Western or Roman Empire, each with its own religious organization. This religious and political split divided the territory of former Yugoslavia into two parts. The eastern part, where the Serbs dominate, fell under the Byzantine sphere of influence, and the western part, where the Croats are in the majority, fell under Rome.

6. After the closing of the educational institutions in Bosnia Hercegovina in 1945, the prospective Franciscans from the region were educated at one of the many Franciscan establishments elsewhere in Europe. In addition, the recruitment of new personnel and other resources occurred (and still occurs) by way of the Croat communities of foreign workers and political exiles in Austria and Germany. In religious as well as other repsects, the communities are almost exclusively led by Franciscans from Bosnia Hercegovina.

7. Nevertheless, the tension between church and state has remained. Among other things, it has to do with an unclear description of the domain of religion. For the state, its domain is limited to purely religious activities, whereas the church, in view of its social responsibility, draws the line as broadly as possible (cf. Alexander 1979; Cviić 1982; Kristo 1982; Petrovich 1972; Ramet 1984, 1985b).

8. In order to get a firm grip on the clergy, which was impoverished after World War II, the state encouraged the establishment of associations of priests. They are a kind of labour union which, using government money, arranges for social welfare insurance and pensions for their members. Against the will of the bishops, who did not want to share the power over their priests with the state, numerous clergy became members. By openly speaking out in favour of the associations and encouraging the establishment of a branch in his diocese, the bishop of Mostar paved the way for further cooperation with the state. In 1950 the Franciscans of Bosnia Hercegovina set up a similar

association called *Dobri Pastir* (The Good Shepherd). Franciscans told the author that they had had two reasons for this: firstly, to demonstrate their independence from the bishop's organization, and secondly, to prevent the state from prohibiting them from working on (former) Yugoslav territory because of their membership in an international religious organization, a measure often taken in young independent states striving for nation-building. It is no wonder the authorities preferred closer cooperation with the diocese. This kind of territorially organized hierarchy is easier to control than an internationally branched network of Order clergy.

9. The establishment of the communist federal state after World War II brought new divisions and antagonisms to a population already divided by nationality. One of the most important was between the state-oriented population in the smaller towns (where party patronage flourished in an over-developed state bureaucracy) and the anti-state-oriented peasantry in the countryside, who lost their independence and, in many cases, their land. They are still one of the most heavily taxed segments of the population. Consequently, hostility toward the state and a revival of the old (Croat) nationalism have developed in the countryside. (For more information on the differential impact of nationalism on (former) Yugoslavian society see: Alexander 1979; Petrovich 1972; Ramet 1984, 1985a, 1985b; Irvine 1993; Banać 1984; A. Djilas 1985, 1991). See also the epilogue of this book.

10. These new priests of the diocese distinguish themselves in many respects from their Franciscan colleagues. Their social manners are characterized by formality and aloofness; they prefer to be referred to as *Gospodin* (mister, master); they emphasize their urban (i.e., superior) background and their scholarliness. The Franciscans, on the other hand, often grew up in the parishes they serve, are warm-hearted and somewhat fervent. In their social manners they are similar to the country folk: they are often called by the kinship term *ujak* (mother's brother), which expresses intimacy, or else 'pater'. One would never call a Franciscan *Gospodin*.

11. This movement, which originated in the United States, can be viewed as a Catholic reaction to the Pentecostal movement. Mystical forms of experiencing faith, and prayer, have an important place in it. The influence of this movement on the fortunes of Medjugorje is said to have been considerable.

12. After Franciscan censorship, the *Gospa*'s messages and instructions are regularly published in devotional leaflets which are then widely distributed in Europe and the United States. According to the 'official' Franciscan reading, there has been a reduction in the frequency of apparitions and messages since January 8, 1987. Since then, only one message is alleged to have been received by one seer, which, after Franciscan censorship, was distributed. However, during my field work, I discovered that it is not unusual for the seers to have some five to eight apparitions per day. They take place in the church, in the homes of the visionaries, and in the fields, where the seers regularly organize religious meetings with pilgrims. Not all the messages are passed on to the Franciscans. Yet many of them reach the people by word of mouth and through the 'grey' publication circuit. (In Chapter Three I show that the messages are, among other things, sources of power in local factionalism between the seers and groups of priests.)

13. That the authorities viewed the phenomenon as a money-maker is also illustrated by their authorizing in 1988 the construction of a big (state-controlled) tourist complex on the edge of town.

14. Informants from the diocesan camp related that the Franciscans had to pay the equivalent of several hundred thousand dollars a year. Franciscans have repeatedly confirmed that 'considerable' sums were concerned.

15. It is indeed true that the bishop defended the apparitions and the then only recently established devotion in an official letter to the authorities (1981). According to Franciscan informants, he still believed that the devotion could be co-opted. In an interview with this author, the bishop of Mostar gave another view of his stance. Initially, he explained, he had been in favour of the movement and the seers, and he still is convinced that the church in general may benefit from the devotion to Our Lady. Only when the youngsters in Medjugorje (allegedly supported by the Madonna) began to criticize his diocesan policy publicly was he forced to take 'other steps'. The prelate concluded: 'After all, the authority of the church is at issue'.

16. Cf. *Glas Končila*, August 16, 1982. According to insiders, the fact that the Conference of Bishops did not completely forbid the pilgrimages has to do with an old rivalry between prelates from the south and the north of former Yugoslavia. More information on this point can be found in Ramet 1985a and 1985b.

17. It was also in this pastoral letter that, for the first time, the diocesan side attacked the authenticity of the apparitions and the integrity of the Franciscans. Ever since, pamphlets have been regularly distributed from the diocese denouncing the apparitions, the Franciscans, and the seers. Copies of all these documents are kept in the archival room of the Medjugorje rectory. Archivist Father Zirko kindly showed the documents, which he half-jokingly called 'war documents', to the author.

18. One of the leading Franciscans in Sarajevo told me in 1987 that according to their calculations at least nineteen of his colleagues had landed in jail for this reason. After paying a ransom, they were quickly released.

19. Videos, films, cassettes with songs and prayers, newsletters, prayer books, brochures with messages from Our Lady, and instruction booklets on how to set up devotion groups for the Queen of Peace are just a few of the forms of propaganda produced at the 'headquarters' in Steubenville.

20. According to one of my sources, a Franciscan from Hercegovina (now working in Germany) who regularly served in Medjugorje, almost 260 such messages had been registered in the parish daybook by mid-1990. From the diocesan side, no figures were given.

21. The religious leaders allegedly refuse to ask money for their goods and services. According to local custom, however, it is impolite to refuse a gift from a friend. A clear picture of the significance of the devotion for the local economy is difficult to present. Up to 1989, the authorities did not openly encourage private enterprise, but the renovation of homes and some newly-built large houses (by relatives of seers) seem to indicate that the hospitality extended to pilgrims has more than just moral considerations.

22. The name *Križari* was used before World War II to refer to the children's section of Catholic Social Action. The task force of the ultra-nationalistic Croatian *Ustaša* Movement in World War II also went by this name. More information about the *Ustaša* can be found in Alexander 1979, A. Djilas 1991, and Krizman 1983b.

23. It is said that *Križari* played a crucial role in the Croat military mobilization in Hercegovina in 1991 and 1992.

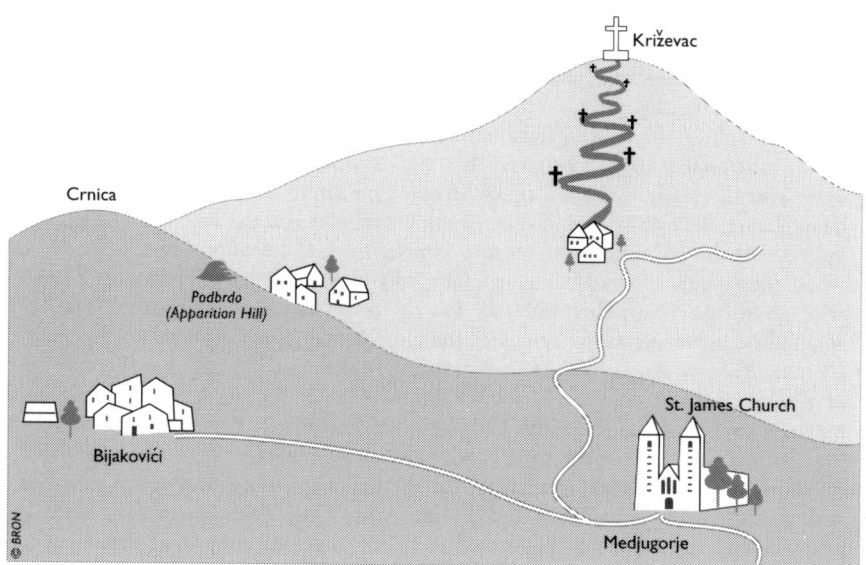

Križevac

Crnica

Podbrdo
(Apparition Hill)

St. James Church

Bijakovići

Medjugorje

© BRON

Chapter Three

Taming the Untamable:
Seers and Management Problems

*'Once an apparition has been endorsed the seer becomes,
in a certain sense, a hindrance to the Church'*. (William
A. Christian Jr. 1973)

Young Seers into Full-Time Religious Entrepreneurs

A few days after the first apparitions, the spontaneous devotion came
to an abrupt end when the police of Čitluk prohibited the meetings and
closed off the mountain of Podbrdo. According to one of the seers, however, the Blessed Virgin made it clear that from then on she would appear
in the church. Thus a period began of daily apparitions in the context of
the liturgical cult.

Perhaps the seers' activities would have remained confined to the daily
passing on of Mary's messages if the devotion had stayed a purely intra-
mural church matter under the supervision of the Franciscan friars. But
the rapidly growing numbers of pilgrims also approached the seers directly, at their homes, which meant an enormous expansion of their tasks.
Almost every day the seers prayed, healed people by touching them with
their hands, and passed on special messages from *Gospa* to persons who
had asked for them. They also had to devote a great deal of time to 'blessing' crosses, rosaries, water from the well near the church and earth and
stones from Apparition Hill. By way of these objects, ever-growing numbers of pilgrims wanted to partake of the 'heavenly powers' they imagined
were flowing down to earth through the seers. These religious activities
soon took up almost all their time and made it difficult for them to continue attending school.

In the long run, not all the seers were able to cope with the pressures. It is common knowledge that one of them stopped seeing the visions after a year, and another after a year and a half. A third moved to Sarajevo and was thus no longer actively involved in the devotion.[1]

Efforts on the part of the Franciscan friars to 'divert' the growing torrent of pilgrims to the church, where the number of daily Masses had increased, did not have the desired effect. The pilgrims continued to seek out the young intermediaries. The seers gradually moved the bulk of their activities from the church and its immediate vicinity to Apparition Hill, which was again freely accessible, and particularly to the homes of their parents. Ever since 1983, the activities of the three remaining seers have developed in such a way that they only take turns attending the evening Mass in the church. They spend their days according to a more or less fixed schedule. A day in the life of Marijana, the oldest (28 years in 1990) and most popular of the seers, may serve as an illustration.[2] In 1983, Marijana dropped out of the course she was taking to become a hairdresser, and ever since then, like her fellow seers Mirka and Janko, she has been devoting all her time to religious tasks.

A Day with One of Gospa's Confidantes

At about eight in the morning, the gate to the substantially renovated farm of Marijana's parents is opened for pilgrims. Earlier that morning, one of the curates has already come to fill the holy water font in a niche of the portal. Marijana's mother and sister and a colleague from the local prayer group Emanvel show the believers (and the curious) the way to a large hall that has been completely rebuilt. At the front, against a white wall, there is a large table with a statue of *Gospa* and several burning candles. When they come in, many people put small objects on the table: rosaries, crosses, handkerchiefs, ribbons, tiny statues, bottles of water, stones and earth from the Podbrdo. They are to be blessed during the apparition of the Virgin Mary. Others hold similar objects in their hands, waiting for Marijana to make her 'round' and transfer the 'power' to their statue, bottle, or stone. The room can hold a good sixty people, and when it is filled, Marijana makes her entrance. She nods in a friendly manner and says, 'Praised be Jesus Christ' in Croat, Italian, English and German. The pilgrims reply with 'In all eternity, Amen'. Marijana assumes her position in front of the table and gives a brief account of how her life has changed since the first apparitions. She summons everyone to pray, to fast, to do penance, to go to Confession in the church and to Communion. Everything she says is translated by several members of the prayer group, who have assumed their positions at the side of the hall. Then the seer asks the ailing and the people with some 'special intention' to come forward, to kneel down and take each others' hands and to pray with her. She kneels down herself on a small rug in front of the table and starts to say the Lord's Prayer. After a few sentences, she stops. It is clear to the audience that *Gospa* is appearing to her. There is absolute silence in the hall. Approximately five minutes later, Marijana goes on with her prayer, radiantly beaming at the white wall where the Virgin Mary is supposed to have appeared. All the people in the hall join her in prayer. The seer stands up and puts her hands on one of the believers in front to convey the 'special grace' of the Blessed Virgin. She tells the audience *Gospa* has heard their prayers and conveys her message.[3] Row after row, laying her hands on the people in the audience, blessing their objects and singing, Marijana leaves the hall. At the door, she personally says farewell to each person and receives 'special tokens of gratitude' from several of them.[4]

It is almost ten o'clock. Outside, the next group is waiting. This time there are also several invalids and people who are visibly ill. They are accompanied by nuns, who are chatting with members of the prayer group. They remember them from a previous trip.

At about noon, when the second meeting is over, Marijana and her helpers rest for a while, although even this recess is interrupted by a few persistent pilgrims. In the afternoon, when the heat of the day has passed, another meeting is held on Podbrdo. These meetings, attended by large numbers of ailing and handicapped pilgrims, make a more improvised impression and often last longer than the indoor ones. Consequently, the seers really have to rush if they want to attend the evening Mass in the church.

This evening it is not Marijana's turn to be at the church. Together with a friend, she answers letters and 'blesses' in-memoriam cards. This current task is rather time-consuming, since numerous people send her requests by mail. Many of the pilgrims who have seen her in person continue to correspond with her afterward.

By eight-thirty, about fifteen people from the village have arrived at Marijana's home. They are members of Emanvel, a local prayer group that holds a closed meeting once a week at the home of one of the seers.[5] As is their habit, this evening they have a meal together consisting of bread, soup and water. After this form of abstinence, they engage in lengthy prayer. Then *Gospa* is claimed to appear to one of the seers. The

Blessed Virgin issues instructions for the group as a whole and for each member individually, which are then discussed.

It is past eleven by the time the members of Emanvel leave the house. Marijana withdraws to pray and to sleep, because tomorrow there will be new groups of pilgrims for her to address.

Franciscan Management Problems and Visionary Confrontations

The Virgin Mary's messages are taken very seriously and are treated with the utmost caution. From the beginning, the Franciscans seem to have been well aware of this. Ever since the first apparitions, they have done their utmost to support the seers and their heavenly messages as best they could and to keep them from violating the doctrines and traditions of the Church. But the religious leaders of Medjugorje were soon confronted with the fact that the supernatural does not always adhere, so to speak, to the rules and regulations of the institutional church. Tensions, conflicts, and disputes between the seers and the priests were among the repercussions.

Places of Grace

The friars followed the rapid growth of the meetings on Podbrdo and at the homes of the seers with mixed emotions. According to one of them, it was not that they felt professional jealousy, although admittedly many of the pilgrims did prefer the mountain to the church; it was just that they felt concern. They were fearful of the government, but most of all they were afraid of the criticism of the bishop.[6] And, indeed, it was not long in coming. In the summer of 1982, a pastoral letter was issued, part of a veritable battle of the pens, in which the prelate of Mostar warned the priests and the congregation about the 'religious decay' taking place in Medjugorje. In the bishop's view, a cult was developing there that was not in keeping with the Canon of the Church and that constituted a threat to the regular services at the church.[7] It is possible that the letter did in fact achieve its goal. It was probably also as a result of the pressure exerted by Rome that the Franciscan priests tried to draw the seers totally back into the church again. At any rate, it was to be some time before there were any more meetings on Apparition Hill. Late in 1982, however, the seers were there again at regular intervals, and in the company of rapidly growing numbers of pilgrims. This intensified the tension between the seers and the priests, which had been latent up to then, but it did not actually come out into the open until the spring of 1983.

One morning (local informants said it was in May), there must have been quite a commotion among the seers and their close friends.[8] On the previous evening, a rather out-of-the-ordinary addition had been made to the collection of messages from the Virgin Mary issued in the past few days and was displayed on the bulletin board next to the church in a wide range of languages. Its tone and contents were very different from those of all other messages. 'Dear children', it said, 'I invite you to turn completely to God and His sacraments. I want more and more of you to always come here and be with me and my son in God's house. I am always here and here the special graces are granted. I want you and everyone else to always receive the Holy Sacraments here, because these gifts of grace are the most important. Pray here without cessation to the most holy sacrament of the altar'.

When they read those words, the seers were totally taken aback. Indeed, one of them got furious, but his elder brother—a key informant of mine—persuaded him to keep calm and quiet. With no ifs and buts about it, the Virgin Mary had made it clear that salvation was only to be received in church via the (priest-monopolized) sacraments. When the clergymen of the parish were questioned, they too claimed to be unable to provide any further information about it.

Whether any open confrontations took place at the parish house at the time is not known, but it certainly did become clear in the next few days that the seers had no doubts about their own task along the road to salvation. For almost two weeks on end, they issued the Virgin Mary's messages from their own homes, and in the evenings they held joint meetings on Apparition Hill. In the church, their seats remained vacant. Again and again, they repeated to the pilgrims what the Mother of God had told them: 'Wherever you are, I am always there too. That is where the special grace will be found'.[9]

These conflicts, which probably were never noticed by the pilgrims, must have come to an end. For some time later, the seers were once again at their seats at the evening mass, though they now took turns.[10] However, the meetings on Apparition Hill and in their homes also continued to be held with undiminished frequency. But new difficulties soon loomed on the horizon.

A Local Prayer Group

The story has it that just before Whitsunday in 1984, one of the seers informed Fathers Ksaver, Krsto and Slobodan that *Gospa* now wanted a prayer group in this parish as well. The Franciscans are said to have been surprised to hear this. They wondered whether the message had been properly understood. They felt that the Virgin Mary would have been sure to announce such an important decision to the other seers as well. And shortly afterwards, she allegedly did just that. The Blessed Virgin stipulated very concretely that the group was to be called Emanvel. The priests, however, still had their doubts. They felt prayer groups were certainly needed in other parts of the diocese. But in Medjugorje, so close to the source, everyone could hear Mary's messages almost first-hand.[11] In short, the clergymen must have decided to interpret the Blessed Virgin's instructions in a different way.

The seers were not in the least discouraged by the fact that the Franciscan friars more or less formally dissociated themselves from the instructions. Indeed, they were convinced they had to carry out every instruction from *Gospa*, including this one. Shortly afterwards, Emanvel was founded. The members, who were initially all relatives and friends of the seers, received a clear order. *Gospa* allegedly told them to help each other and to support and stimulate the seers in announcing and propagating her messages. They were also to serve as a helping hand for the needy among the parishioners.

Emanvel proved to be clearly viable. There was a steady rise in the number of members and it expanded its activities among the parishioners, a development the Franciscans kept a close watch on.

'Seers of the Second Generation'

The concern on the part of the Franciscans was not completely unfounded, since Emanvel was indeed soon to constitute a regular source of antagonism and tension in the parish. Its members have even been said to make quite a profit on the apparitions, to have gotten themselves 'cushy jobs' and, together with the seers, to be 'getting rich' on the pilgrims. They are also said to have established lucrative connections abroad.[12] Less critical local observers do not deny these accusations, but they immediately add that all this has enabled members of the prayer group to do a lot of good for many a parishioner.[13]

In their effort to restore order and unity to the parish, the Franciscans received a very unexpected kind of assistance. On March 19, 1985, the

36

feast of St. Joseph, two new seers emerged from the ranks of Emanvel: Branka (12) and Jelica (13). These 'seers of the second generation', as they are generally called in religious circles, had received overtly clear messages and instructions from the Blessed Virgin. Father Vjekoslav gave the following account: 'Branka came to tell me that the Mother of God wanted me to be present during the apparition she was going to see at her home. Jelica was also going to be there. That afternoon I went over there and after the prayer I was present during the apparition. Then Branka told me that the Mother of God wanted a new prayer group which She was going to lead Herself and which was therefore to be named after Her. It was the express desire of the Blessed Virgin that a priest also be a member of the group.[14] *Gospa* also especially recommended including youngsters in the group. Every member would have to bring a new member every week. Whenever possible, they all had to attend Holy Mass'. Comparing the two groups of seers, Father Vjekoslav made the following comment. 'Branka and Jelica have received a clearly complementary charisma and I maintain that we priests are closer to them. For us, they signify more hope than the other seers'.[15]

On June 24, 1985, exactly four years after the first apparitions in Medjugorje, the new prayer group called Marija was consecrated in the church. The group consisted of eighteen members, fourteen former members of Emanvel and four new youngsters. Before the congregation of the believers, all the members testified to their faith in the Virgin Mary. They also promised to honour God's sacraments, to obey His servants (the priests), and to unselfishly love humanity.

The prayer group, the new seers and their priests must have had a stimulating effect, since it was not long before a majority of the children of the parish were members of Marija.[16]

Full Circle?

By the middle of 1988, peace seemed to have been restored on the religious front in Medjugorje. Marija had come to occupy a strong position in the parish. Its most important activities included the weekly prayer meetings in the church, where the Virgin Mary's messages to the new seers were announced, as well as the support of the needy and elderly of the parish, the maintenance of the buildings and grounds of the church and the provision of plants and flowers for daily church services.[17] Emanvel, plagued by the apparitions of the opposition, and numerically reduced, managed to survive. Its visionary leaders retained their 'monopoly' on the apparitions during the evening mass in the church, and the group as a whole concentrated its attention on welcoming and supervising the pilgrims.

Early in 1989, however, it became evident that the 'cease-fire' in Medjugorje was to be short-lived and that there were new problems in store for the Franciscan friars. By then the pilgrims had already 'discovered' the seers of the second generation. Steadily increasing numbers of pilgrims were asking the new seers to intercede for them with the Virgin Mary. The young seers were unable to cope with the tremendous moral pressure by themselves. With increasing frequency, they had to call upon friends and relatives to help them deal with the numerous problems presented to them. It has been with growing concern that the Franciscan friars have observed these developments. They want to avoid a repetition of what happened with Emanvel, or perhaps an even worse situation.[18] Troubled and uneasy, Father Krsto described (1989) the supervision of the Medjugorje devotion as 'taming the untamable'.

Conclusions

The priests of Medjugorje have constantly been confronted with two related types of management problems. Firstly, they have had to prevent the seers from starting to operate more or less independently, since they would thus become a threat to the priests' position as spiritual leaders of the parish and the devotional movement. Secondly, they have had to keep the seers from speaking out or behaving in any way that could compromise their reputation or discredit the devotion itself.

The professionalization that took place among some of the seers was not so much an effect of the seers deliberately aspiring to power; rather, it was forced upon them, so to speak, by the pilgrims. Pilgrims are, in the first place, confessors of a practical religion that provides solutions to physical and other personal problems. For this purpose, they focus on holy places, and more specifically on individuals in whom they feel that heavenly power directly and tangibly manifests itself (Christian 1973; Turner and Turner 1978; Stirrat 1992; Eade and Sallnow 1991). It was the pilgrims who were thus primarily (though not intentionally) responsible for the development in Medjugorje of a group of alternative religious specialists with their own cult, who regularly came into conflict with the official leaders of the parish.

A similar development took place once again relatively soon after the emergence of the second generation of seers. In no time, these young persons were also 'discovered' by the pilgrims and encouraged to engage in an independent, professional application of their special gifts, thus losing much of their significance as a strategic weapon for the local clergy. Pilgrims apparently make it almost impossible for the institutional church to incorporate practicing seers permanently and completely into its regime.

The pilgrims were also of great importance to the seers' role development. They soon transformed the bearers of heavenly messages into intermediaries in a two-way communication system between mortals and the supra-terrestrial. In the eyes of the pilgrims, this extensive contact with the sacred world also meant an accumulation of heavenly power in the seers themselves. This power could be easily 'tapped' (by touching and by laying on of the seers' hands) or 'stored' (in crosses, rosaries, water, earth and stones) and then regularly summoned at home. Thus, the seers increasingly came to resemble folk doctors, persons who had been quite common in rural Europe in the past (Bouteiller 1966). The steadily growing influx of pilgrims made it necessary for the seers to seek the help of assistants. This added still another new element to their role. They became local employers: leaders of a staff of employees of an 'enterprise' focused around a visionary cult.

The cult itself exhibited a clearly analogous development. Prayer and heavenly messages, once virtually its sole components, were gradually overshadowed by quasi-medical acts, aimed towards curing ailments and restoring health. Any further 'medicalisation', however, or growth of the cult toward total independence would seem unlikely. The state would pronounce an alternative medical organization or a new religion as being in violation of the law, and would take drastic steps to oppose it. More important, however, such a development would not be in keeping with the two-sided religious orientation and allegiance of most of the believers involved, the pilgrims and the seers alike. Pilgrims, after all, are not only part of an international circuit revolving around seers and other charismatic personalities, a circuit in which 'extraordinary revelations' play a central role; they are also the product of an institutionalized and formalized church culture. Likewise, the seers of Medjugórje are not only the result of a pilgrim-oriented culture; they are also part of the institutional church. This is why consolidation of the existing relations and maintenance of the present-day hybrid nature of the cult—a mixture of 'magic' and elements of Christian rituals—would seem to be most logical.

That this kind of configuration of double dependencies and orientations necessitates compromises and ambivalent behaviour was also evident from the conduct of the priests toward the seers. To maintain their own position in the religious arena, the priests stimulated the seers. On the other hand, to keep their position they were continually forced to curb and correct the seers' activities. The fact that they thus entered into a coalition with the new seers should not be viewed as overly narrow-minded involvement, but as a direct consequence of their two-sided position.

In closing, a few comments on the messages and instructions from the Virgin Mary. These 'words from heaven' not only served a function for the believers; they also appeared to be a function of the power relations in the religious arena of Medjugorje. The alternating emphasis on the cross and Apparition Hill, on the one hand, and on the church and the sacraments on the other, as representing different paths to salvation, reflect the rivalry and the delicate balance of power between the contesting parties. The messages also functioned as instruments of power to force a particular type of behaviour upon one's opponent. The perpetually repeated closing phrase, 'Thank you for coming' not only expresses gratitude, but also forces the seers to regularly come to the church, the opponent's centre. These observations seem to indicate that one can also improve one's understanding of the dynamics of devotional movements by systematically studying the heavenly messages in terms of power and dependence. Further research, especially regarding historical movements which are sometimes well-documented though only theologically interpreted, will bear that out.

Notes to Chapter Three

1. Since 1989, the third seer is back again in the summer season and claims to have visions once per day in her newly-built summer residence.
2. The information was obtained through participation and observation in 1986 and 1988. During later field work, only minor changes appeared to have taken place.
3. The message for that day contained an instruction *Gospa* had given before: 'Dear Children, today I once again ask you and everyone to put more religious objects in your homes. Also carry sacred and blessed objects with you as a shield against Satan's attacks'.
4. What is involved here is money given by people from abroad. Villagers say this happens every day.
5. These meetings are for members only and priests are not admitted. The reason for this will become clear in the next section.

6. One should bear in mind that until 1989, public religious meetings could only be held at spots specified by the state and 'interpreted' by the local authorities.

7. More details are to be found in Craig 1988 and Žanic 1990.

8. The information that follows is based on discussions with a key informant who is a close relative of one of the seers.

9. Another message was also circulating at the time, one that was overtly clear. 'Dear children, the cross is also according to God's plan, the cross you have set up on the mountain. [This is not Podbrdo, but Križevac, another mountain, selected by the priests -- MB.] Go now more than ever to the mountain and pray at the cross. The gifts of grace will be overwhelming'.

10. It is striking that ever since then, in the church the messages from the Virgin Mary have always ended with the words, 'Thank you for coming' (Cf. Blais 1985, Laurentin 1986, Ramet 1985).

11. This information was given to me by a Franciscan friar, a Croat, who had been a priest in Medjugorje for some time but now works at a Croat mission abroad.

12. According to my Franciscan informant, the other friars were apprehensive about any further growth of the seers' influence. When Emanvel was set up, my informant said, a more or less permanent staff was created, making it possible for the meetings outside the church to function better. It will become clear that this explanation is not totally unfounded.

13. The controversial prayer group is alleged to have close links, financial as well as otherwise, with a well-known, world-wide Roman Catholic lay movement, which has been responsible for a regular influx of pilgrims.

14. This claim would seem to have been confirmed by the recent renovation of many of the houses and stables and the purchase of new farming equipment. Indeed, all the close relatives of the seers have profited considerably from the religious tourism. In 1993 all of them had built impressive modern houses, some of them with swimming pools and other luxury features. Local jokers call this residential area Little Hollywood.

15. Cf. Brunner 1986. I have absolutely no reason to suppose that local priests have deliberately manipulated the children in any way. The emergence of new seers in a region that has been characterized by a visionary culture for some time is not an unknown phenomenon in anthropological literature. See e.g. Boniface 1966, Gabriel 1968, Maclin and Crumrine 1973. However, this does not exclude the possibility that the priests of Medjugorje might have viewed these new seers as a useful instrument in the solution of their management problems.

16. By the end of 1988, according to the priests, almost all the Confirmation candidates in the parish, more than 100 children, belonged to the prayer group.

17. These messages from the Virgin Mary are said to be received earlier in the day and then discussed with the officiating priest, who incorporates them into his sermon in the church. It is striking that these second-generation seers never see an apparition in the church. According to some of my Franciscan informants, however, this is only a question of time, as is the further growth of the ranks. Among Medjugorje clergymen, there is the firm conviction that 'at a given moment' there will be a total of five new young seers.

18. During the recent war, antagonism came into the open. The houses of the seers of the second generation were damaged. In 1993, one of these seers, Jelica, told me that they were convinced that 'the others' (relatives of the older seers) had had a hand in it. She argued that it could be no coincidence that in all cases only the guest rooms had been

damaged. When discussing this with Father Krsto, the priest did not want to give any details; he just remarked that 'Satan had left no family untouched'.

Chapter Four

Going for Grace, Fighting for Spoils: Religious Patronage

'Theory and concepts in anthropology should be tested in the analysis of life as it unfolds in some particular place in the world. So any such place can serve as a provocation to challenge and criticize anthropological theory'. (Fredrik Barth 1989)

Little more than two years after the first apparitions, hardly a day went by without pilgrims coming to see the visionaries. With the help of their relatives and friends, the seers made every effort to cope with the growing influx of people seeking their help. Virtually every day, each of them held several 'services' in rooms of their parents' homes. But this still was not adequate. The pilgrims, who did not always have a great deal of patience, had to wait outside until it was their turn to go in. Enterprising villagers took advantage of this opportunity to earn a bit of money and sold bread, fruit and drinks to the pilgrims. According to village standards, there must have been quite a chaotic hustle and bustle, which was not to the liking of the still-vigilant police. The story goes that the pilgrims were repeatedly fined for disturbing the peace, as were the vendors for selling without a licence. Anyone who failed to pay the fine was put into temporary custody in the nearby town of Čitluk.

The seers and their helpers sought a good solution to the problem. They felt they had found the answer in what was later to become known as the *zajednacki sistem*.[1] Local persons especially selected for this purpose, almost all of them close agnates, would regularly pay visits to the private addresses where the pilgrims were staying (up to the end of 1989, the construction of hotels was prohibited by the government). In consultation with the guests and after discussing the matter with each other, they would draw up a schedule for the 'services'. The pilgrims were to gather in small groups at the colossal church square, where it was usually extremely crowded, and were then to be unobtrusively taken by a *zajednac* to the home of one of the seers, which was approximately fifteen minutes' walk from the square. The system was not effective. The regular police force, and the secret police that was up to 1991 inconspicuously on the scene, soon discovered what was happening. The *zajednaci* were fined, as were many pilgrims, for violating the law against religious processions. 'So we were back at square one', a former *zajednac* concluded. However, a more permanent solution was soon to emerge from an unexpected quarter.

Secular Interference, Monopolistic Organization

In 1983 it was already clear to the (former) Yugoslav travel agencies, all of which were indirectly supervised by national authorities, that religious tourism of sizeable proportions was developing in Medjugorje.[2] Two of them, Kuna Tours and Envas (both from Bosnia Hercegovina) had managed to secure a licence to organize excursions for the 'tourists' who were staying in Medjugorje (another agency already had 'claimed' a monopoly on transporting the pilgrims to and from Medjugorje). In spite of the advertisements at the church square and in their town offices, business was not going well. Very few pilgrims were interested in an excursion to an old city, a waterfall, or any other sights. And the foreigners who came with their own buses sometimes organized excursions themselves. But the enterprising agents did not take no for an answer. They contacted some former *zajednaci*, and in exchange for a regular supply of pilgrims, they offered them attractive positions in their organization—'and a share in the profit', as an indignant Franciscan friar added to me.

In small communities, it is difficult to keep anything secret for long. The seers and the *zajednaci* who were not approached soon heard about the plans. This group, the core of the later prayer group of Emanvel, was upset and indignant. They viewed it as a downright takeover. Soon everyone, seers, *zajednaci* and pension owners alike, would be totally dependent on Kuna Tours and Envas. The repercussions would be disastrous. They implacably refused to have any further contact. However, as an informant once commented during a long talk on the subject, 'even black water can wash a mountain clean'. What he meant was that even hostile parties can profit from each other. The checkmate the authorities' steps confronted the seers and their helpers with at the end of 1983 forced them to reconsider and negotiate. The formula the parties arrived at was surprisingly simple (but also 'beneath their dignity,' as a Franciscan priest angrily informed me). In exchange for a regular supply of tourists who went on an excursion of a certain price with Envas or Kuna Tours, the agency would transport the pilgrims to and from the home of one of the seers escorted by a *zajednac*. The latter were to have the sole right to sell the tickets to these combination excursions. Both parties would thus profit from the arrangement: the travel agencies would have customers, the seers and their helpers would not be hindered by the law prohibiting religious processions, and both parties would retain a large extent of autonomy in their own domains. (As a reaction to the arrangement, in their sermons the Franciscans put even more of an emphasis on Christ and the sacraments.)

This curious symbiosis did, however, force the seers and their helpers to adopt a firmer organization structure and a stricter division of functions. Emanvel soon became the 'headquarters' of the new patronage network. The permanent staff there has since consisted of four seers, ten *zajednaci* (each of whom is linked to a group of about fifteen boardinghouse owners), two people who answer letters and two people who coordinate the cultic meetings. The team also includes several interpreters and a bookkeeper. Working together with enterprises operating under the aegis of the national authorities had thus necessitated a better-organized body to participate in the economic field.[3]

Medjugorje's 'Sindikat' as Observed in 1990

On the outskirts of the village, *Pansion Medjugorje* is a modernized home that can house twelve paying guests. The boarding house is run by an elderly couple and their son, Mirek, and his wife, who also live there. One evening early in May 1990, at the start of the pilgrimage season, twelve Dutch pilgrims had just arrived. Like most of the pilgrims, they were going to stay for one week. They had barely settled in when they immediately started asking what time they could meet the seers. Mirek's mother said the seers were extremely busy, but that 'a friend' of theirs would be coming the next day who might be able to help. During breakfast the following day at the boarding house, a man came in, Janko Sirol, a former mechanic at Mostar Airport. In German—he also speaks English—

Janko told them that almost all the pilgrims wanted to meet one of the seers in person. That used to be easier, but the enormous influx of pilgrims and the strict government measures had made it virtually impossible. At that time it was only in combination with an excursion approved of by the authorities that they could meet one of the seers at his or her home. This week there was an excursion to the old city of Mostar on the programme. The excursion cost about twenty dollars. In addition, there was a small expense fee of about fifteen dollars. Janko apologized and made a vague allusion to 'the rules' that were 'different' in this part of Europe. The pilgrims could sign up with him for the excursion. That evening he would come and tell them when there would be seats available for them. Almost all the pilgrims immediately signed up for the excursion, some of them mumbling under their breath about all this state intervention—even after communism!

The next day at lunch, several pilgrims talked about how they had tried in vain to find some other solution. The two tiny offices of the travel agencies had not been much help, and at the church they had heard that there really were no alternatives. One of the Franciscan friars had told them emphatically that they could observe the seers every day of the week at evening mass, but there would be little chance of having any personal contact with them on those occasions.

Janko returned that evening. He had managed to reserve seats for them two days later. Without exception, all the pilgrims now signed up for the excursion. Janko wrote down their names and after they paid him ('preferably in dollars, German marks or Dutch guilders'), he gave them a *karta naročit*, a ticket with a special note on it and his signature.

Two days later, just before six in the morning, an Envas bus stopped in front of the boarding house. Janko, who personally welcomed and checked the twelve pilgrims as they got into the bus, told them that first they had to go and pick up two other parties, a Dutch one and a German one, so that in all the group was to consist of more than forty pilgrims. During the trip to Mostar and back, the 'tourists' were escorted by an Envas official, a woman wearing the travel agency uniform. Janko did not take over until they were on the way back to Medjugorje. On behalf of what he called 'the community of Emanvel', he now welcomed the passengers as pilgrims and no longer as tourists. He told them they were about to arrive at the home of Marijana, who would receive them with joy. He gave them instructions on how to enter and what to do with the objects they wanted to have blessed. He also gave them a rough description of what the session was going to be like. Lastly, he urged them not to leave the house until the bus had arrived again.

The session, which was centered on the prayer, the meeting with the Mother of God and her 'special grace', went according to plan. Barely an hour later, the pilgrims were on their way to their lodgings. During dinner, there was much to say; everyone in *Pansion Medjugorje* enthusiastically affirmed that the 'gifts of special grace' had been more than worth the expense. A talkative lady told the others how she had expressed her gratitude by putting an extra 'little something' in the collection box at the exit of Marijana's house. It turned out that others had followed her example. Completely contented, they went to bed—except for this author, who had been among this group of pilgrims, and Mirek, who had long been one of his prime informants in the village.

The young boarding-house owner told me about the latest developments. Mirca had returned from Italy several months ago, so there were once again four seers 'at work'. Two *zajednaci* had gotten good jobs in the United States through a rich American pilgrim, leaving Emanvel without a bookkeeper. Since Mirek had worked as a bookkeeper for a company in the nearby town of Čitluk (a job he lost as a result of his involvement in the devotion), he had been asked to fill the position. All the *zajednaci*, Mirek told me, had once had good jobs but lost them for the same reason. The authorities had not been making much trouble lately. But they were not willing to issue more than the existing 130 boarding-house licences to private persons. The local authorities in Čitluk, the *komune* to which Medjugorje belongs, were still prohibiting the construction of hotels in Medjugorje.[4] So for the time being, the local people were still in charge as far as accommodations were concerned. One of the *zajednaci* had gone abroad to do some fund-raising because, according to Mirek, the excursions did not bring in enough money to live on. 'We have our boarding house ... but the others ...'. He calculated that Emanvel was host to about 1,500 pilgrims a week, divided between about 130 boarding houses with an average capacity of ten beds. For every excursion that was booked, they got approximately fifteen dollars. About five dollars went to the boarding-house owner and the rest had to be divided among the ten *zajednaci*, the seers and the other people on the staff. In spite of the extra donations, which Mirek did not want to say anything more about, he still felt it was not nearly enough. The *zajednaci* are each responsible for the guests at thirteen houses every week, which is a total of about 150. And each seer receives about 325 pilgrims a week, divided over some eight sessions. Smiling, he concluded his account with the words: 'The *sindikat* is good, but the *ekonomija* can use a bit of improvement'.[5] After very piously wishing me sweet dreams, he said goodnight.

Discussion

Eric Wolf has advocated a more systematic study of what he calls 'parallel structures', such as patron-client relations in complex societies, as these would augment our understanding of the dynamics of these societies (Wolf 1966). Wolf's suggestion has been taken to heart in the political field, but for religion it has barely met with any response at all.

The preceding description seems to indicate that Wolf's proposition is applicable to the religious field as well. Indeed, similar networks centered on visionaries have developed elsewhere in Europe and overseas as well; they operate more or less permanently between the institutional church and its authorized devotions on the one hand, and the secular authorities on the other.[6]

These human configurations could be characterized as patron-client networks. They fit into the generally accepted notion of patronage, neatly summarized by Boissevain (1977) as 'an asymmetrical, quasi-moral relation between a person (the patron) who directly provides protection and assistance (patronage) and/or who influences persons who can provide these services (brokerage), to persons (clients) who depend on him for assistance. Clients, in turn, provide loyalty and support when called on to do so.'

In what respects do these visionary-centered patronage networks differ from patron-client networks in the political field? Firstly, in terms of role development of leading personnel. For the seers, this development can be characterized as patronization. From go-betweens and brokers dealing in 'second-order resources' (messages and sacred contacts), the young Medjugorje seers increasingly turned into patrons who dispense 'first-order resources' (sacred powers more or less permanently located in themselves). Similar developments have been recorded for seers in Mexico (Macklin and Crumrine 1973), Portugal (Vissers 1989), Italy (McKevitt 1988; Satriani and Meligrana 1982), and France (Auclair 1968). In the field of active politics this kind of transformation takes place to a very limited extent as it is rather risky. Boissevain observes in this connection: '... conversion is tricky, for by becoming also a patron, the broker becomes unequivocally tied to his promises to make his first-order resources available. Unless he is able to dispense these to his clients, his credit diminishes rapidly ...' (Boissevain 1974: 162; see also Mayer 1966 and Paine 1971). In short, political leaders in clientelist contexts remain first and foremost brokers.

Visionary-centered patronage networks also differ from political patron-client networks in relation to resources. Unlike political leaders vis-a-vis their clients, seers deal primarily in resources that are not scarce in an objective sense. Special grace, blessings, supranatural power and heavenly love can all be handed out without diminishing one's resources. This is probably a basic reason for the difference in role development between seers and politicians.

A third point to be mentioned is about competition, which appeared to be minimal between the seers of Medjugorje. Indeed, they even joined forces to form a more or less durable united front—a picture that also emerges from descriptions of other seers elsewhere (cf. McKevitt 1988, Macklin and Crumrine 1973, Vissers 1989, Satriani and Meligrana 1982). This stands in sharp contrast to leaders of political patronage networks, who always seem to compete with each other openly or behind the scenes. Here again the nature of the resources seems to be an important factor. For each of the seers there is always an adequate supply of blessings, grace and supernatural power to distribute among the clients. There also appeared to be little need for the seers of Medjugorje to compete for clients, since there were always enough for all of them; indeed, there was a potential surplus of clients. This takes us to the next point: strategy and client mobilization.

For the continuation of their office, leaders of political patronage networks must strive to maximize their clientele and to optimize their accessibility. To further these ends, they introduce 'social relays', persons who more or less continuously keep in touch with a leader and his or her followers (cf. Bailey 1969; Bax 1976; Boissevain 1974; Scott 1970; Weingrod 1968, 1977). Leaders of visionary patronage networks, on the other hand, seem to adopt a strategy aimed at limited access, by means of introducing 'social resistances'. The *zajednaci* in Medjugorje are a case in point, and persons with similar functions have been described for other visionary movements (cf. Vissers 1989, McKevitt 1988, Satriani and Meligrana 1982). Classical examples of this strategy are to be found among the desert fathers and stylites of Syria and Asia Minor (cf. Brown 1982).

More could be said about visionary patronage networks as opposed to patron-client networks in the political field. In the latter the interpersonal relations are usually described as mainly transactional or instrumental (they are 'quasi-moral', not really moral!) In the Medjugorje case, on the other hand, they seem to be basically moral but also contain important instrumental elements. Pilgrims and seers exchange primarily moral values but also material ones, such as money against blessed stones or holy water. It may be said that pilgrims visit the holy place to meet the Lord, but at the same time they want some special, private help. It should also be emphasized that 'going for grace' is not a 'one-shot affair', as F.G. Bailey once observed.[7] Just like political clients, a seer's followers require more or less continuous servicing. Many make regular trips back to the holy place, and they keep in touch through private communication, newsletters, and messages received via prayer groups at home. Also, they come back in large numbers when called upon by the seers' heavenly messages—to celebrate a particular religious feast, at the same time publicly demonstrating the 'strength' of their patrons (cf. Craig 1988). These, then, are some of the ways clients 'provide loyalty and support when called on' (cf. Boissevain 1977: 81).

Moral and instrumental elements also characterize the relations between the core-members of the visionary network of Medjugorje. Boarding-house owners, *zajednaci* and seers depend on each other for work and income. At the same time, however, they are related through kinship and friendship, they participate in the same local prayer group, and many of them have approached the seers to ask for their interecession with the Virgin Mary in cases of serious problems in their personal lives or those of their families. Only the personnel of the two travel agencies, though recognized as being of vital importance, fall outside this category. Indeed, these five persons are outsiders: they come from other towns and are not reckoned to belong to the local patronage group.

In closing, it may be postulated that visionary-centered patronage networks constitute a unique combination of moral and instrumental relations. On the one hand, they combine elements from the institutional church and its theology with patron-client networks in the political field. On the other hand, they are sufficiently different from both to approach them as a relatively autonomous field of inquiry. Systematic and cross-cultural research is certainly needed for conceptual refinement. At the same time, however, this parallel structure may improve our understanding of religious dynamics in complex society.

Notes to Chapter Four

1. In the local language *zajednac* (plural *zajednaci*) means one who binds together; it is a term from tobacco farming. Originally a *zajednac* is a softened twig that ends in the shape of a hook, which is placed around a batch of tobacco leaves. Held together this way, they are transported and hung in the sun. These twigs can in turn be easily bound together and transported. There is a saying in the area: 'Without a good *zajednac* there is no good tobacco'; in other words, you can not achieve an end without the proper means. This new meaning of *zajednac* has become common knowledge among the population of Medjugorje.

2. A detailed description of former Yugoslavia's complex political, legal and economic structures is given in Ramet 1985. Here it may suffice to observe that up to the war in 1991, Yugoslavia's travel organizations were self-managed collectives; direct state intervention was limited. On the other hand, only members of the League of Communists had any chances of obtaining (good) jobs in those quasi-independent organizations. As a result of this party patronage, which was claimed to be widespread and which cut across the boundaries of the former constituent Republics of the Federal State (cf. Djilas 1957), it will not surprise anyone that many people in Medjugorje equated business and good jobs with the party and with the formal authorities of state and government.

3. The economic details are still not quite clear to me (and probably never will be). An official from Kuna Tours claimed in 1990 that, by order of the government, Emanvel was given the legal status of a cooperative organization, which enabled the government to calculate and tax its share in the excursion revenues. Several of the *zajednaci*, whom I do know quite well, said this status is not final yet. In the legal field, they claimed, there was still a dispute going on as to whether a prayer group, as part of the church, is a charitable institution, which is largely exempt from taxation. These *zajednaci* also informed me that the revenues received all went into a common fund, from which the boarding-house owners were paid their share, and the rest of which was divided on an equal basis among the members of Emanvel. It was also said, particularly in Franciscan circles, that this excursion money was only a fraction of the much larger sums that came in from individual pilgrims and prayer groups abroad. Systematic research on this point is perhaps too much to even hope for.

4. Later in 1990, the local government declared Medjugorje 'free market'. Shortly afterward, the 'local war' broke out; see also Chapter Eight.

5. Another current term besides *sindikat* is 'conservative Mafia' (cf. Craig 1988, Cviić 1988, Tanner 1988).

6. For example in Ireland (Corish 1985), France (Beevers 1953, Bloys 1970, Estrade 1899, Guilhot 1973, Auclair 1968), Spain (Gabriel 1968), Mexico (Macklin & Crumrine 1973, Watson 1964), Italy (Boniface 1966, McKevitt 1988), Portugal (Vissers 1989), Peru (Sallnow 1987), and Sri Lanka (Stirrat 1992).

7. Personal communication.

Chapter Five

Haunted by Priests, Pilgrims, and Devils: Women of Medjugorje

*'... [u]ncritically accepting an arbitrary male viewpoint
... has impeded study of women and of private domain.
... [w]e are caricaturing 50 per cent of the Mediterranean world'* (David Gilmore 1982)

Ruža, who is fifty-five, has spent all her life in Bijakovići, near Podbrdo. Together with her husband, their two sons and
their daughter-in-law, they have turned their home into a small boarding-
house. As a result, farming has become of secondary importance to them.

For a number of years, Ruža has been having a hard time of it. It is
difficult for her to cope with the domestic work and she often complains
of fatigue. She tends to be agitated, has unstable moods and fits of depress-
ion. She barely ventures out into the street and seems to have become
afraid of people, especially other women in the village. She consulted the
doctor in town, but there was nothing much he could diagnose. In his
opinion, Ruža is overworked and ought to try to take it easy, and her
husband and sons are of the same opinion. Yet Ruža is convinced something very different is going on. At regular intervals, she hears voices, she
foresees accidents and other calamities near and far away, and she has the
feeling that slowly but surely she is being sucked in by *Crna Moća*, the
Black Power.

Ruža is not the only one in the parish with experiences of this kind.
She says some of her relatives and a number of other women have similar
problems. All of them say that more and more women are confronted
with the same kind of thing. The men call it *ženska histerija*, women's
madness. They do not set much store by those fairy tales, and they are

backed in this respect by the local clergy—though they do have to admit that ever more women are starting to act a bit sickly and *strane* (odd).

The first doubts about this established male perspective began to rise in the 'objective' mind of this male author in 1989, after a relatively unimportant incident. In the heart of the pilgrimage centre, I witnessed a traffic accident. A taxi driver hit a German couple walking arm in arm along the curb. The woman was swept along by the car and banged her back against a wooden electricity pole. Bleeding and unconscious, she lay on the street while the taxi slipped off the side of the road and landed in the dry bed of the Lukoc River. Oddly enough, her husband was completely unharmed. A circle of people gathered around the unfortunate woman. When the disconcerted taxi driver, a young man from the village, came scrambling up the hill, he was stopped by an old woman perilously waving a shepherd's crook. She shrieked that this was already his fourth accident. Did he need any more proof that the devils were now all over and were even attacking the 'guests' (as the pilgrims are usually referred to)? A loud discussion ensued, a shouting match of men against women. A police patrol car arrived. Witnesses were requested to come forth, and I was one of the people who complied. We were all taken away in a police van and questioned for the rest of the day at the police station. In the course of the talks I had there with several women, I began to realize that 'women's madness' constituted in fact a complex world of representations, experiences, perceptions and behaviour patterns of the female segment of the community; a world, as I discovered during the research that followed, of devils and evil spirits that were increasingly terrorizing the women in the parish.

This chapter describes this female world and the conditions and mechanisms the women hold responsible for the outburst of the devils' activities. An effort is then made to explain this demonology and the related behaviour in sociological terms.

The Middle Field: Hidden Powers of Good and Evil

From one generation to the next, the people of Medjugorje learned from their spiritual leaders about the Middle Field, a region situated between God and the Devil at one end and earthly mortals at the other. The Middle Field is the realm of good spirits and evil ones, saints and devils, who engage in fierce battles on behalf of people, frequently on their request, and regularly demonstrate the outcome of these battles on earth.[1] The story goes that in dreams or visions, people sometimes even venture into the Middle Field. The priests are said to be regular visitors there. Priests do, however, occupy a special place: by way of the sacraments they are capable of conveying the goodness of God to all humanity. In addition, they can use divine powers to exorcise devils who have taken possession of largely innocent people.[2]

There has always been quite a lot of coming and going in the Middle Field, or so the story goes. At regular intervals, people have also been confronted with what they viewed as spontaneous descendings of good and evil spirits. This was claimed to be the result of the never-ending battles between devils and saints.

There is generally a relative equilibrium in the relations between people, devils and saints. But in stressful times, during wars or feuds, it is profoundly disturbed.[3] Then evil powers can easily gain the upper hand. More than a decade ago, when there were portents that the Mother of God was to appear in Medjugorje, the equilibrium was disturbed, but in a positive way.

Ruža recalls about that period: 'Our priests were often at the Middle Field, and many of us [women] felt we were there as well. It was as if the Black Powers were shrivelling ... like leaves in a fire. We felt ourselves becoming stronger, less tense and more tranquil inside ... like the dusk. Our priests—we had two of them at the time—gladdened us with the message that the Mother of God looked after us in a special way. Everything became even better, even stonger inside when *Gospa* came to us. They (the secret state police) were very hard on us, but *Gospa* gave us strength and she laid an impenetrable screen over us. And all those people (pillgrims) who came to look and wanted to hear what we had to say ... that was wonderful, it gave a warm feeling. In those first few years, we had so much strength ... we could cope with everything: the work on the land, the goats, accommodating the guests, the Masses. No one was really ill and no one left (died). The guests said we were as radiant as *Gospa*'.

'But that much goodness could not last forever', said Janja, Ruža's neighbor and sister-in-law.

The residents of their hamlet became painfully aware of this when Janja's grandson met with his tragic death. Janja was at work on the plot of land next to her house, which bordered on the Lukoc River. Her four-year-old grandson had been living with her for more than a year because the air was so much healthier than in the mining town where his parents lived. In this way, the child could be closer to Our Lady. By dinner time, the boy still had not come home. Later his body was found floating among the poles of the fish nets. The accident was interpreted in a religious sense. Perhaps, the people of Bijakovići conjectured, *Gospa* was not strong enough after all to counter the evil powers of the Middle Field. In the years to come, this question was regularly posed by more residents of the rapidly growing pilgrimage centre. The priests, however, were of the opposite opinion, explaining that setbacks, tensions, and accidents were in keeping with the rapid expansion and the great attraction of the pilgrimage centre. But more and more women in the parish gradually began to think differently.

The first reason for this change was probably a series of accidents in the hamlet of the Šivrić clan. In the early autumn of 1984, Vlado Šivrić returned from what was then West Germany with the money he had saved there. Despite the objections of his wife, Vlado and his two sons began to convert the family home into a small boarding-house. Vlado is a cautious man who generally avoids taking risks. Despite all precautions, he fell off the scaffold and broke both ankles. While working with the concrete mixer, his sons were later both seriously injured. It is true that with the help of several neighbours, the work was completed in the end and the men did recover from all the accidents, but then Vlado's wife fell ill. She began to complain of devils following her around all the time, ruining the food she was making, hurting and frightening her. The same devils, she was certain, who had first caused her husband's fall and her sons' accidents were now after her.

In early 1985, two virtually identical accidents occurred in the hamlet on the other side of Apparition Hill. Once again, men were the immediate victims but in the end it was the women who continued to suffer from ailments they felt were the devils' doing. Ever since then, a veritable psychosis has developed among the women of the parish. By May 1989, the priests at the parish hall had received more than three hundred reports of ailing women and approximately the same number of requests for excorcism.[4]

Ruža and her sister-in-law Janja were indignant at the ease with which the priests of the village dismissed this growing problem as *histerija* and refused to exorcise the devils. They both believed this was why a number of women sought the help of several *kalajdzije* in the vicinity. *Kalajdzije* are wise old women who traditionally have been consulted, much against the wishes of the local clergy, for advice in the event of illnesses 'of the head' or 'of the heart'.[5] Ruža and Janja informed me that in the past few years, quite a few women in the parish have been advised by these traditional medical-religious specialists. The means of protection include amulets and talismans worn on the body, branches and bundles of herbs and pieces of metal attached to the corners and openings of houses, gardens and fields, under the head and the foot of the bed, behind toilets, in supply cupboards and near cattle in the barns. The purpose of all this was to ward off the devils—who the wise women were sure were causing the trouble—and to break their diabolic power and keep them from settling permanently in the bodies of the women. Ruža and Janja also knew that various women had been advised to be careful of certain other women in the parish and in fact to stay away from them completely, but they were not willing to reveal any further details in this connection.

It was not only in dramatic ways but also in everyday occurrences, the informants said, that the devils made their evil presence felt with increasing frequency. The breaking of a whetstone when mowing the grass, the splitting of tobacco binders, the wandering off of a goat, the souring of milk, the spoiling of eggs, the breaking of a dish, the burning of a meal; these are only a few examples of the things the devils did.

And yet—as other women repeatedly stressed as well—it was not true that all domestic mishaps and local accidents could be attributed to devils. Negligence, carelessness and pure clumsiness were also accepted factors in the women's interpretation of the world. It was only in the event of very specific physical experiences that a devil was certain to be involved. One would hear or feel a soft rustling breeze, though not a single leaf or twig, not a single hair of the dog or feather of the chicken would move, just like before a storm. Some women claimed to have then experienced a feeling of general fatigue, lethargy or paralysis, whereas others sensed a severe tightness in their belly and thighs, and still others said their hands grew numb or could not move. Almost all the women reported breaking out into a cold sweat which lasted for some time.[6]

There is a fairly general consensus as to what is apt to happen next. The experiences described above consitute the first stage, the duration of which can fluctuate from a quarter of an hour to perhaps several hours. Tiny little demons are thought to be involved, evil creatures that wander about quite freely, and can cause only a relatively limited extent of damage or inconvenience. Should the sensation last longer and become more intensive, this leads to a growing suspicion that a *mučan vrag* (heavy devil) might be involved, either operating independently or on behalf of some nearby human being with evil intent. Women are particularly fearful of these devils, since they cause much more damage and may also attack close relatives. (The drowning of Janja's grandson and the construction accidents were viewed as examples of demonic interventions of this kind.)

There can be a transition from this stage to the last and most feared one, during which the devil permanently takes possession of someone. Women are then perpetually ill and present a continual problem for themselves, their families and communities. Many women fear this will someday happen to them, but despite all this, none of the informants would mention one single example of permanent possession.

Explanations: The Women's Perspective

The women agree that the sharp increase in mental and physical ailments among the local females is related to the recent development of Medjugorje as a pilgrimage centre. But not one of them accepts as a possible explanation the enormous increase in the amount of work they have to do. The very notion is immediately refuted with the argument that they were also very busy in the past, and that they often used to work even harder because the men and boys were away. The sharp and continuing rise in the number of devils is the current explanation among the women, and they mainly blame the priests and the pilgrims for this development. Ruža's interpretation was very explicit: 'When *Gospa* came', she said, 'she brought a great deal of good. But wherever there is a great deal of good, there is also a great deal of evil. Our priests have taught us that themselves: where special grace is great, evil seeks its prey'. And to stress the religious authenticity of this view, she added: 'In Her message (to Marijana), Our Lady cautions against the devil and his sly ways ... the Middle Field has become full, completely full. *Gospa* brought her angels— the guests left their devils behind here. They fetch milk and they leave blood, that is the way we see it here. And blood attracts more blood. More devils, the little ones and the heavy ones alike, more and more of them are out to find a place for themselves in the Middle Field. But that is full. That makes them even more vicious and angry. Now they are looking for their place in our midst; a lot of them remain here'.

Ruža made it clear that she cannot actually blame the pilgrims for coming; after all, they cannot help wanting deliverance from their misery. But it certainly did not please her that the guests were so focused on their own problems and failed to pay any attention to those of the parishioners. Her opinion on the seers and the priests was much more outspoken. She could become especially agitated and upset about the priests because, in her opinion and in that of many other women, in the beginning the priests could have steered the demonic forces in the right direction. With a *delegacija* of nine women (one from each hamlet), Ruža told me she went to the parish house to protest, which in fact was an attempt to demand a solution.

What Ruža told me one evening in the presence of several other protesters about the confrontation with Father Jure also reflected the different world views of the local peasant women and the Franciscan priests trained in contemporary theology: 'Father Jure, what happens if you see a dead goat lying in the field? Aren't more and more wolves drawn to it, and don't they attack each other, wound each other and even tear each other to bits? The cadaver and the dead wolves have to be removed. Because otherwise blood will continue to flow. And that is also the way it is with human beings and devils. If the priest does not pray and swear over the person possessed, then the devil goes on ranting and attracting other devils and possessing other people'.

In short, systematic exorcism would keep the evil forces under control. That was the opinion of Ruža and the other women at the time, and it still is today.

Father Jure, Ruža said, felt it was a well put comparison, but he did not think it applied to what was going on. He pointed out that in former times, women would be exorcised by his colleagues and the devil would thus be driven out of the community. But nowadays not a single woman was really possessed—that was a point all the priests and all the men in the parish were in agreement on. Father Jure also said one should not look for the Middle Field outside oneself, and according to the women nowadays all the young priests feel one should seek it inside oneself. Every individual has a Middle Field where good and evil contend. And it is only by way of prayer and God's grace that good can emerge victorious. That is why women ought to go to confession more often and go to church to receive the holy sacrament. Father Jure also stated that he and his colleagues were well aware of the seriousness of the problems so many women in the parish were confronted with. They were looking for ways to more frequently bring the women close to God ... in the church.[7]

Disillusioned, the group of women returned home. They all felt their priests had not come through for them. 'It has been some ten years now ... *Gospa* and the priests are for the guests ... And what about us? We have to be strong, they tell us. But how? Like animals in the woods in the cold of winter? That way the wolves are certain to find us!' Ruža's lamentation is typical of the self-diagnosis of many in the village.

A Sociological Perspective

Why do many Medjugorje women perceive their fate as described above, and why are the related experiences increasing so rapidly? Two social processes seem to be relevant in this connection: first, the sharp decreasing social status of many women, and second, the rapid growth of the pressure exterted by the pilgrims.

In the period prior to the apparitions and immediately afterwards, women constituted the most prominent group in the parish. The prayer groups and other religious activities were an example of highly esteemed piety. It was widely felt that without their efforts—whether or not they were led by the priests—the Virgin Mary would not have appeared. In short, women were widely respected by the clergy and lay people alike, and they were clearly aware of their special position. However, they soon had to relinquish this high rung on the social ladder to the seers and the parish leaders, who were now in the limelight all the time. The women were largely forced back into the domain of the home and had little choice but to tend to the material needs of the pilgrims.

The rapid expansion of religious tourism made it possible for many of the men working elsewhere in Europe to return home. They not only took command of the family and the farmwork, they also engaged in economic activities related to the pilgrimage centre. Women who for years had been in charge of their farm and family had to stand by and watch their position being reduced overnight to that of a subservient house-keeper.

At the same time, the multifarious pressures were exerted by the pilgrims on the residents of Medjugorje. It is true that the pilgrims provide the mainstay of the parish economy, but it is equally true that they thoroughly influence the social and psychological life of the population. 'Everyone has to work harder and the priests insist we all do our very best to make a good impression. The guests always have to be able to see the effects of the special grace on us', was the way one of Ruža's fellow protesters formulated it.[8]

This pressure led to inner and interpersonal tensions. Due to the constant presence of the pilgrims, however, even the slightest sign of tension always had to be camouflaged and suppressed. Various escape strategies were available to the men. Whenever they wanted, they could leave the *sveti krug* (sacred circle), a term men often use to refer to the parish. Up to 1991, the men paid regular visits to a larger town in the vicinity to get drunk and let off steam. They also went off to the mountains to do some shooting, or so they claimed. But escape strategies like these were not available to the women. Not only did they have to see to all the material needs of the pilgrims day in day out, they were also expected to serve as religious examples. Priests' sermons reinforced the conviction widespread among the pilgrims that women of the parish occupy a special position and perform a special task in God's plan of grace.

Together with the total lack of any satisfactory regulatory mechanisms, these forms of social pressure may clarify why ever more women suffered from increasing anxiety and stress. The demonological interpretation of these feelings has been unwittingly reinforced by the parish clergy's conduct and stimulated by the advice and activities of the wise old women, the *kalajdzije*.

How was it possible for such a strong preoccupation with demonic powers to develop among the women, while nothing of the sort was evident among the men? In general, the belief in devils and witchcraft is thought to be related to social tensions (cf. Cohn 1975; Geschiere and Van Wetering 1989; Marwick 1982; Moore 1987; Taussig 1987; Thoden van Velzen and Van Wetering 1987, 1989; Thomas 1971). In this part of the Balkans, particularly in Bosnia and Hercegovina, extreme social tension has long been a virtually structural phenomenon. In addition to wars and civil wars, until very recently this kind of tension was mainly caused by the almost endemic conflicts and feuds between and within kin groups, which easily ended in violent vendettas.[9] Women, land, cattle and the distribution of water constituted the most important motives. Men had the sole right to solve these conflicts by way of physical violence. To a certain extent, men could thus deal with their own tensions by way of open aggression. For the women, who were often the underlying cause of the conflicts and thus had good reason to experience quite a bit of stress themselves, in this part of ex-Yugoslavia there was no similar way to openly regulate tension and let off steam. The tension accumulated and led to forms of hysteria and other psychosomatic symptoms. These symptoms were diagnosed in a demonic idiom, a system of religious representations that gradually developed into a compromise between indigenous beliefs and Roman Catholic doctrine. Popular religious specialists and their Roman Catholic counterparts played roles in this connection, both believed to have the capacity to keep a check on the devils or exorcise them. This was to the advantage of both parties involved. The women got the attention they wanted and their signal was clear: up to this point, but no further. The religious specialists, on the other hand, thus confirmed and reinforced their own positions.

Possession and exorcism also fulfilled a social function within the larger community. In this society, where the monopoly over the organized means of physical violence has never been effectively established, priests were the peacemakers. Urged on by the insistence of the women who were ill, priests made every effort to bring disputing parties closer together, after which exorcism could take place. In short, possession and exorcism were also instruments to keep men's violence under control.[10] It is perhaps relevant in this connection to note the saying: 'A strong women is like a warm cooking pot, a filled crib and a clean cowshed; a sick women deprives her husband of his strength and his honour'.

It is this combination of social and individual pressure that makes it clear why the women developed such a pronounced demonology and the men did not. It was in the women's interest to keep a check on conflicts, whereas men were forced by their code of honour to regularly engage in acts of violence. The belief in devils, however, would discourage acts of this kind. That is why the men were so unlikely to believe in any interpretation involving devils. This makes it easier to understand why, as far as the belief in devils is concerned, up to this very day the women and the men are still living in virtually separate worlds.

Conclusion

Demonologies reflect inner and interpersonal tension, provide ways to channel them, and can also serve as instruments of power. The eruption in Medjugorje of the fear of devils can largely be attributed to the pilgrims' presence, but its origins are in a more distant past and have to do with power relations between the sexes. In this male-dominated society, the possessed behaviour of women not only channeled their inner tension, it also served to restrict the private use of violence by men. Wise old women and, even more importantly, local priests played a crucial role in the process as interpreters of behaviour and as ritual peacemakers. In short, the physical violence of the men was kept in check by the women through the use of religious or quasi-religious power.

There are some indications that similar mechanisms played a role in other Mediterranean societies with a weakly developed state-monopoly on the use of violence (Black-Michaud 1975, Boehm 1984, Cozzi 1910, Denich 1974, Engel 1798, Wilson 1989, Whitaker 1968). In Mediterranean anthropology, however, it is not unusual for micro-politics and physical violence to be discussed quite separately from such problems as the sources of religious forms of expression (cf. Davis 1977). Should further research bear out a more general pattern, this would open up new perspectives on an old problem. Various researchers (e.g. Christian 1972, Davis 1984, Pina-Cabral 1986) have drawn attention to the prominence of Mediterranean women in religious practice, whereas the official Catholic doctrine only grants them a restricted formal position. In pursuit of an explanation, the authors have worked from the perspective of the clerical authorities, who make every effort to reinforce their influence on society via women, the least-powerful group. This explanation is undoubtedly important, but the Medjugorje case would seem to indicate that it is only one side of the coin. Women make just as much use of the clergy to reinforce their own influence in society.

In conclusion, there is one more general, programmatic point. In the past decade or so, there has been increasing interest on the part of sociologists, historians and anthropologists in the study of witches, magicians, devils, demons and other evil figures and forces. There is a growing conviction that, rather than being obsolete, this 'dark' problem area is in fact very topical and relevant to today's western and Third World societies alike (e.g. Geschiere and Van Wetering 1989, Luhrmann 1989, Thoden van Velzen and Van Wetering 1988, De Blecourt 1990, Marwick 1982, Taussig 1987). The case discussed here would tend to support this conviction, though it also calls for a cautiously astute approach and conscientious comparison. Witchcraft accusations, convictions and prosecutions are frequently mentioned in the same breath as possession by devils. The recent outburst of fear of devils in Medjugorje and its historical manifestations bear virtually no similarity to the witch plagues and witch hunts in other parts of Europe and elsewhere. These are different phenomena with different meanings and functions. In the case of witch hunts, the interests of the 'prosecutors' play a crucial role; an increase in witchcraft is not necessarily involved. In the past and the more recent collective Medjugorje delusion, however, it is neither a matter of accusations nor of persecution. It concerns a means for weaker members of society to channel emotions and keep a check on conflicts and violent behaviour. In short, in endeavouring to develop a general theoretical perspective, ample space should be left for the formation of more specific interpretative frameworks.

Postscript

During short visits in 1991 and 1992, several local people told me that women's madness had intensified. I could not systematically investigate this since many women had been evacuated and taken refuge in Germany. Moreover, pilgrimage had virtually come to an end. My 1993 trip ended abruptly when a warlord, who destroyed my films and written records, forced me to leave the area.

Notes to Chapter Five

1. The metaphor of the Middle Field is found in many peasant societies. In this particular case the world is constructed of three layers or fields: *Nadzemlja*, the world above where God resides; *Srednja zemlja*, the Middle Field; and *Poljana* or *Zemlja*, the field of the earth's surface, where people live. Koljević (1980) provides a striking explanation of why Franciscan friars stimulated these old local beliefs and practices. See also Balić 1992.

2. In addition to this exorcism, in the past priests also gave their congregation advice and provided them with consecrated metal objects and herbs to keep devils at a distance and prevent them from possessing people. Later in this chapter, it will become clear that the present-day priests of Medjugorje, almost all of whom were educated abroad, have a rather reserved and ambivalent attitude toward these ideas and behaviour complexes.

3. This region has frequently been the site of violence: on the part of the Ottoman Turks up to approximately 1870, the Hapsburg troops up to 1918, and the Serbs up to approximately 1925. A civil war between Serbs and Croats raged there in the interbellum; during the Second World War there were German and Italian troops; and then the Partizans until after 1950. Usually the attacks were short but violent. In the hamlets, women and children would be murdered and property either stolen or destroyed. Many of the men fled into the mountains and made guerilla attacks on their enemies' home areas. In addition to these forms of warfare, vendettas and blood feuds were endemic in the region. This makes it easier to understand the development of a violence-oriented mentality among the male segment of the population. The provincial archives of the Franciscans in Duvno also contains a great deal of relevant and rather shocking information about the use of violence in this region. During the recent war in Bosnia Hercegovina, Medjugorje was also the site of large-scale violence. More details will be given in Chapters Seven and Eight.

4. This information was given to me by one of the clergy responsible for parishioners' spiritual care. A closer analysis, conducted in conjunction with a colleague of his who had a university degree in social science, showed that it was mainly married women and widows who provided accommodation for the pilgrims. The fear of possession by devils, however, was much more widely dispersed in his view, and occurred among younger women and girls as well. I was able to talk about this topic with 41 of these women distributed over nine neighbourhoods. With only very few exceptions, the girls were barely responsive, if at all. In one or two cases, the mother served as spokeswoman.

5. *Kalajdzija* (plural: *kalajdzije*) literally means coppersmith. It is a half-Turkish word which, like so many Croat words and sentence constructions, has been 'turkicized' in this region. Coppersmiths often used to belong to a peripheral ethnic group. Like the gypsies with their widely ramified social networks, these people also literally lived on

the edge of the peasant communities. Their women were said to have 'the gift of sight'. According to my informants, they used to be the overt rivals of the priests, and they too could exorcise and provide metal amulets and protective herbs. Since the founding of the Communist state in 1945, and up to 1990, the work of these women has been illegal and far less multi-faceted as the government had a monopoly on medical and paramedical care. The priests call these wise women *gatare* (single: *gatara*), which means heretics. The women themselves are said to prefer the term *proročica*, the Croat equivalent of the clairvoyant women in Classical times.

6. See note 4. All these informants said they had learned the interpretation of this experience from their mother, grandmother or some other female relative. Many of these conceptions, they said, were then shared by the former parish clergymen.

7. Father Jure, who remembered this conversation with Ruža and the other women, did indeed view the problems as disturbing. He was of the opinion that tensions were increasing in many Medjugorje households. He felt, however, that they could be viewed as a kind of 'growing pain' and he therefore advanced a variant of the modernization thesis that changes in the parish were taking place extremely rapidly and women were having an especially hard time coping with them. He felt that, given sufficient time, the problem would pass. Father Jure held that exorcism would not provide a solution. (He failed to mention, however, that the government had in fact declared it punishable by law!), as there were no traces of true, permanent possession by devils. What was more, in his opinion and in that of his colleagues, exorcism might very well backfire. The women would see it as a confirmation of their views, which would only lead to an increase in the number of requests for exorcism. In addition, the priest continued, the country's Synod of Bishops had been urging the local clergy to exercise the greatest restraint in connection with this and other such age-old customs.

8. This statement is inconsistent with what the women said on prior occasions about having to do so much more work. And yet there are no traces here of an ethnographic error, but indeed of quite a normal sociological phenomenon: people say different things, perhaps even contradictory things, in different contexts. In other words, alternative discourses are involved.

9. Cf. note 3.

10. The Duvno archives clearly illustrate this, as do the parish records in Medjugorje. Eruptions of violence almost always coincided with a rise in the number of requests from women for exorcism. In cases where this assistance was granted, the accounts often include the words 'Da bi se umirila krv' (so that the blood may be pacified). I have not yet been able to find any further details on the preparations for or the actual exorcism ritual. Like the local women, the present-day priests are extremely reluctant to provide any information on this subject. It is striking, though, that Serb communities had an extensive ritual, the *Slava*, for settling feuds.

Chapter Six

Holy Mountains: Sacralization as a Political Process

'... we ... are led to believe that the order we see is not of our own making, but rather an order that belongs to the external world itself'. (David Kertzer 1988)

'But Mister, this just *is* a holy place!' a panting lady from Holland snapped at me as we ascended the Križevac. She had overheard part of my conversation with a Dutch colleague about how the mountain had come to be a sacred place. The woman's reaction reflected a notion that is virtually universal among pilgrims. It holds that the world consists of two separate domains, the sacred and the profane. Even among scholars in the field of religion, this is an established view. It can be traced back to influential sociologists like Emile Durkheim or Mircea Eliade, who refers to the sacred and profane as 'two modalities divided by an abyss' (1954: 14). This prevailing view has nonetheless been the target of criticism. Evans-Pritchard (1956) and Malinowski (1925), for example, observed that this dichotomy was far too rigid and failed to leave any leeway for situational flexibility. Recently, John Eade and Michael Sallnow endorsed this view when observing that 'the sacred and the profane exist as categories created by different interest groups who define boundaries according to the social groups to which they belong' (1991: 13). Others have criticised the static nature of the established approach, in which the sacred is viewed as a given. They have propagated a dynamic approach centring on the genesis and evolution of sacred representations and practices (e.g. Asad 1983; Douglas 1982; Firth 1981; Kertzer 1988; Lukes 1975). In short, it is this process of sacralization rather than 'the sacred' that should be the subject of study.

This chapter elaborates upon this view and examines the sacralization of Križevac, the mountain that came to occupy such an important position in the complex of ritual activities at Medjugorje. At a more general level, it attempts to promote the systematic study of sacralization in conjunction with secularization.[1]

Sacralization can be conceived as an aspect of religious regime formation, more specifically as a strategic instrument. Specialists within these regimes utilize this instrument to establish and consolidate their powers. Sacralization implies defining an object, a phenomenon or an element in the landscape in religious terms and underpinning this definition by way of ritual activities. Specialists endeavour in this way to further a sacral monopoly. Their strategy aspires to impose 'their' definition and the ritual activities it entails on as many people as possible, excluding all the while those of other specialists and laymen within other religious regimes. Although sacralization is performed by religious entrepreneurs, in its outcome it is equally determined by unanticipated conditions and unintended effects of these religious entrepreneurs' actions. Thus sacralization should be viewed as a relatively autonomous process with its own dynamics.

Christianization of Grmljavinac (1340-1460)

Since time immemorial, people have been convinced the Trtla Mountains are inhabited by spirits and anthropomorphic powers (cf. Vego 1981; Soldo 1964; Djordjević 1953). The intentions of these beings are not apt to be kindly, but the conviction is widespread that sacrifices can molify them. Gromovnik, the spirit of thunder, is still feared. From his refuge on the Šipovac, which the elderly still call Grmljavinac (Mountain of Thunder), he can go into a veritable rage of fury. In the heat of summertime, he routes gushes of scorching fall winds into the valley causing spontaneous fires, and in autumn his devastating hailstorms are equally feared.

The people of Medjugorje have always suffered severely from Gromovnik, since they live closest to the heat of his breath, but in the adjacent part of Bijakovići, his deeds have also long made everyone shudder.

In 1337, Franciscan priests came to this region at the request of a Bosnian monarch. They were confronted with a relatively extensive ritual aimed at averting the dangers and appeasing Gromovnik (Quaestio 1979). In the 'dangerous season', the clan elders of Medjugorje would climb the mountain. Uttering incantations, they would sprinkle water and strew young plants and young fruit. Once they arrived at the top, they would sacrifice a young sheep or goat. They closed the ceremony by lighting fires around the peak.

It is hypothesized that the origin of these representations and practices—the pre-Franciscan sacralization process of the mountain—is linked to a religion of the Bogumiles (Vego 1981; Soldo 1964). Bogumilism was an early 'heretical' movement that had dominated parts of Bosnia and Hercegovina, as is evident from the numerous colossal gravestones (*stečći*) that can still be seen in the region (Fine 1975; Balić 1992). Early Franciscan observations, quoted in *Quaestio* (1979), seem to support the hypothesis. Medjugorje, with a number of gravestones, was indeed a Bogumil religious centre at the time; none of these giant stones have ever been found in Bijakovići. For the performance of the ritual, *Quaestio* informs us, the people of Bijakovići had to rely on the family elders of Medjugorje, whom they paid for their services. If, however, the ritual failed to have the desired effect, *Quaestio* tells, the villagers of Bijakovići would take reprisals. The antagonism between the two villages could be heated, and destruction of personal property and even manslaughter were common.

One of the first tasks of the Franciscan missionaries was to obliterate this religious regime, which they felt just served to sow dissension, and to establish their own regime. Instruments used in this process sometimes bore a resemblance to those of modern-day Peace Corps workers. They taught villagers to build their houses of stone so they would not go up in flames as easily. They helped villagers cope in times of drought by digging deeper wells and saving water in cisterns. They also taught them to plant rows of cypress trees as natural windbreaks for their fields. They organized a warning system and set up mutual aid groups to help extinguish fires. Another aspect of their strategy was focused on incorporating the holy mountain into their own regime. Two facets are striking in this connection. Firstly, they shifted the ritual midpoint to the family units within the villages. This resulted in a mixture of clan ancestor worship and Roman Catholic rituals.[2] Secondly, on the Catholic holidays they organized processions to Mount Šipovac to venerate Christ, God and the Virgin Mary and invoke their protection.

The Franciscan Christianization campaign was particularly successful in Bijakovići. In Medjugorje, however, the builders of the new regime met with opposition from the established religious specialists, whose power position was undermined (Vego 1981; Quaestio 1979). It nonetheless looked as if a prominent 'paganistic' place of sacrifice to subdue the forces of nature was being transformed into a Roman Catholic place of worship.

The Ottoman occupiers soon put a stop to this. Around 1460, these empire-builders reached the northwestern border area of their empire. They closed off the mountain to the local population and used it as a military stronghold.

Ottoman Rule and Rehabilitation for Gromovnik (1460-1870)

The Turkish rule was long, severe, and at times cruel. But the Turks were also opportunists, implementing a policy mainly aimed at the extraction of maximal surpluses (Cole 1981, Drobnjaković 1960, Balić 1992, Malcolm 1994). The Franciscans, always versatile and resourceful, ingeniously tapped into this. In exchange for organizing and guaranteeing the regular payment of tribute, a number of priests managed to gain a certain extent of latitude in the religious field. Backed by the 'Muslim enemy', they were thus free to build up their own religious regime in Bijakovići, including a churchyard and a chapel. But the war economy of the sultan was a demanding one, and as soon as the Brotnjo seemed to have been pacified, a similar agreement was made with the other 'party'. For a regular remuneration, which they recouped from the population, the clan elders of Medjugorje were granted the sole right to hold ritual meetings on Mount Šipovac in honour of Gromovnik. Repeated efforts of the Franciscan friars to undo this 'injustice' were all in vain. They did manage, for a certain fee, to get permission to administer the sacraments at the homes of the Medjugorje villagers who requested them. According to Franciscan sources, this enabled clergymen to keep some manner of foothold in what had now become the territory of their opponents (Quaestio 1979). In this fashion, the divide-and-rule policy of the Turkish occupiers contributed to the rise and long-term perpetuation of two local religious regimes, each with its own sacral centre and both characterized by limited expansion potential.

Serb Penetration, Ethnic Violence, and the Genesis of Mount Križevac (1875-1941)

In the last quarter of the nineteenth century, the Ottoman Empire suffered a rapid decline. Due to internal problems and external pressure, it had to relinquish more and more of its territory. At the Congress of Berlin in 1878, the Austro-Hungarian empire gained control over Bosnia, a province rich in raw materials, and the adjacent province of Hercegovina. Geopolitical considerations played an important role in this usurpation. The Hapsburgs were wary of the Italian interest in this part of the Balkans because the Croats, who were then strongly represented in the western part of the region, had traditionally felt more closely associated to the culture of ancient Rome. In order to keep the usurpation drives of other states in check, the Hapsburgs stimulated a migration movement that had already gained momentum among the Turks. They thus promoted the further development of a multi-national society, which would be more difficult to incorporate. In addition to Austrians and Slovenes, Serbs were the main group to settle virtually throughout Bosnia and Hercegovina as farmers and tradesmen with the capital they had accumulated. This meant a considerable reinforcement of the Serb element in the ethnic patchwork.

According to elderly informants, it must have been around the turn of the century—and the archives of the Franciscans in Humac confirm this—that a group of newcomers settled on fallow land on the border between Medjugorje and Bijakovići. Members of three clans of Serb shepherds had purchased a sizeable strip of barren land there and the right to water their cattle at the nearby Lukoc River from the Hapsburg authorities. For the tiny community of Medjugorje, it must have been an ominous invasion. History proved them right: ethnic differences date back to that period and set the tone for almost half a century of social, political and religious life.[3]

Time and again, the large herds of sheep and goats broke loose and damaged the crops of the local Croats. Dissension and irritation were also caused by the Serb longing for a sacred place of their own. Local sources have it that they offered money to the elders of Medjugorje to build a church of their own on the Šipovac's lowest slope, but the plan did not materialize.[4]

New opportunities opened up for the Serb community in Medjugorje after the fall of the Hapsburg Empire in 1918, when the Kingdom of Serbs, Croats, and Slovenes was founded. In 1929, the (Serb) king abolished all democratic institutions by way of a coup and replaced them by fervent anti-Croat functionaries who were backed by the Četnići, a militant Serbian division of the state police. With official support from Četnići, the Serb community in Medjugorje was able to confiscate farmland. The land allegedly belonged to people who had either joined or at any rate sympathized with the newly founded Croatian Farmers' Party, a political organization that aspired to greater independence and the improvement of the position of farmers, many of whom were in a wretched situation due to the rapidly penetrating money economy and the escalating economic crisis (Bičanić 1936). Part of the hard core of this party consisted of *Ustaši*, the later adversaries of the *Četnići*.

Supported by the expansionist government, the Serbs in Medjugorje launched a new 'assault' on Mount Šipovac. This time it was successful and a house of prayer, albeit of modest dimensions, was built on the mountain. A Serb Orthodox religious regime thus seemed to have been formally established. But that was not all. Djure Smoljan, a Serb merchant who had made his fortune elsewhere, had settled with some of his relatives in the centre of Medjugorje. He provided his local fellow tribesmen with groceries and acquired the sole right to purchase *mošt* (grape juice) and grain from local farmers. Smoljan became an extremely powerful man, and it was on his initiative that plans were made for the construction of a Serbian Orthodox monastery at the foot of the Šipovac. Local opposition was firmly suppressed with the help of *Četnići* and as construction work began it looked as if Mount Šipovac would become the centre of a dominant Serb religious regime. Added to the confiscation of land and economic exploitation, this too served to make a fertile breeding ground for the *Ustaša* movement (which has to have a major nucleus in Medjugorje in World War II). The movement became the organizational hub of the resistance in the area against the 'foreign invaders'. The destruction of Serb property, mutilation of individuals and even manslaughter were soon to be everyday occurrences. The Serbs responded in kind, sometimes with even greater violence, and were backed in the process by mobile units of *Četnići*. Quite a few people fled, and especially the Croats sought refuge in the United States and Canada, where they later supported the cause by donating money. 'It was like in the Krajina of today', an elderly respondent informed me in the summer of 1991. He had lost four brothers during this period, and he added that his family was not an exception in this respect.

The trials and tribulations of violence and economic crisis were made even more trying by three years of drought (Bičanić 1936; Maček 1957; Soldo 1964). In an interview about this 'black period', Janko Babić, young chaplain of the parish at the time, observed: 'The time was ripe for a divine intervention'. What he was presumably trying to say was that the Franciscan leadership felt ready to intervene and to establish hegemony over other religious regimes. Babić continued: 'Father Brno, the leading priest of the parish, was summoned to Rome in 1932. In a dream, Pope Pius XI had been told to build a huge cross on the highest mountain in

Hercegovina in honour of the 1900th commemoration of the crucifixion of Christ. According to the Holy Father, having this cross in the vicinity would mean salvation for numerous believers'. The pope promised the priest financial backing for the execution of the task. After he returned home, Father Brno conveyed this message to the people. 'Everyone was yearning for the drought to end, and since it meant extra earnings for all and sundry', Babić added matter-of-factly, 'almost everyone joined in, even a couple of Serbs'. A building contractor was hired and almost every day, young and old came together to chop stones and carry them 1200 metres up the steep mountainside, along with the mortar and water and whatever else was needed for the construction of the cross. A year later, the fourteen-metre-high edifice had been completed. 'And from that day on', Babić concluded, 'nature has never again produced the same kind of disastrous effects'. An annual procession of prayer to the mountaintop, which was renamed the Križevac in 1933, was set up. This is how Franciscan hegemony was once again established and how the mountain came to signify reconciliation and unity (under Catholic supervision).[5] Gromovnik's regime seemed to have disappeared from the public sphere once and for all, and has been confined since then to the private, domestic sphere. And the Serb regime was not to survive for long, as will become clear below.

Tito's Star Shines Everywhere (1941-1981)

The following decade brought large-scale traumatic changes. With the support of the Axis powers, the Independent State of Croatia was founded, and the *Ustaši* were soon in control. Officially supported by the Roman Catholic clergy in the beginning, this movement implemented a 'Croatization' policy that outdid the *Četnići* in pure cruelty (Petranović 1963). All the Serbs who lived on Croatian territory had to disappear; it was an outright massacre.[6] In the Brotnjo region that was part of the new Croatian state, the *Ustaši* were equally ruthless. The Brotnjo was 'swept clean' of Serbs, as an ex-member of the *Ustaša* put it in 1991. He accompanied his words with the gesture of someone brushing dirt off his hands. The despised aliens were driven together at a spot near the hamlet of Šurmanci, a few kilometres from the village, the story has it, where they were shot and tossed into the ravine.[7] Medjugorje was 'liberated' from 'the other race'. But the region had to pay a vast price. Groups of *Četnići* later attacked the Croats in much the same way, and later still it was

Tito's Partizans who 'pacified' this *Ustaša* hotbed with unforgettable brutality.[8]

In theory, these horrendous times came to an end when World War II was over and Tito established his regime. But the former Partizans who took over the administration instituted a veritable reign of terror in the Brotnjo. My informants have repeatedly told me that barely a family in this part of the plateau survived the atrocities unscathed. Incarceration, torture, rapes, confiscations: these were only a few of the horrors of the Partizan reign. Even the Roman Catholic clergy, who had certainly not remained on the sidelines during the bitter tribal battling in World War II, suffered severe losses. Of the clergy who had not fled the country, many were massacred by Tito's men. Together with part of the local population, the priests of Medjugorje toiled on the Titovac, the name the Šipovac went by at the time. The monastery and the church of the Serbs were demolished, and the villagers had to use the stones to build a five-pointed star, the symbol of communist Yugoslavia, on the old plinth of the razed cross at the top of the mountain. The Titovac became a state shrine where the 'heroes of the people' were annually commemorated under the supervision of Communist Party bosses. Anyone who failed to attend these ceremonies ran the risk of a jail sentence or worse.

The Queen of Peace Chooses Her Own Mountain (1981-1984)

Incited by the conduct of the Partizans newly in power, and often aroused by disputes about rights to land that had formerly been confiscated by local Serbs, the old clan feuds flared up again in the 1960s and 1970s.[9] Old Vida Pavlović's case is one of many vivid and sad illustrations. In spring 1978, Vida was in the vegetable garden next to her house in Bijakovići spreading manure that had been carefully saved. Her neighbour and a nephew came to inform her that her youngest son, her darling, had been found at the nearby well, his throat slit. He was the last surviving son; her other two sons and husband had been killed in the Second World War and her only daughter was still missing. Vida knew right away who had done it and despite her age she swore to get revenge; her nephew was a witness to this. No longer bound to life by family ties, she went out with her husband's rifle and shot the man who had murdered her son, then killed herself.

In political and religious circles in the region, the explosive expansion of private violence was taken to be an alarming development. It was particularly menacing for the local church leaders, the Franciscan friars, who were seen by the government as foci of subversive movements. Bishop Žanić, on the other hand, saw it as a pretext for the expansion of his own sphere of influence and a way to further reduce the power of the Franciscans, the traditional opponents of the diocesan administration. Chapter Two has dealt with this intra-church rivalry, its background and the pacifying effect of the Franciscan regime; here a different aspect is relevant. For the promotion of a devotion, a sacred place is usually, though not always, called for (cf. Eade and Sallnow 1991). Mount Titovac, invested with an immense sacral value, had been placed outside the religious domain by the Tito regime and thus could not be activated, which is why the Franciscans aimed at Bijakovići. Mary not only appeared on Bijakovićian territory; via a series of messages the Holy Virgin also informed her audience that Podbrdo (second in height only to the Titovac) was the place she would sanctify (Rupčić 1983). 'The Queen of Peace chose her own mountain', one of the local priests observed.

Thus a new type of shrine emerged: a holy 'station' visited daily by the Virgin Mary, who conveyed her messages and instructions to an international audience.

Križevac Retrieved: Sacral Expansion and Differentiation, (1983-1991)

The mass influx of pilgrims did not fail to affect Bijakovići. In no time, a considerable portion of the population had made good money. The seers and their families also managed to considerably improve their position.

No wonder the people of Medjugorje, the village on the other side of the valley, could not witness all this without envy and jealousy. All the old antagonism was in the air again. The church and the parish may have been on Medjugorje ground, but most of the pilgrims wanted to stay as close as possible to Apparition Hill. The people of Medjugorje sought ways to get a share of the revenues coming from religious tourism.

The situation altered in their favour with the emergence of the 'seers of the second generation' dealt with in Chapter Three. It is alleged that these youngsters, living at the foot of the Titovac, also received messages from the Holy Virgin. Indeed, as described, they took over the role of their predecessors: at the church, in receiving guests, and in having their messages spread to an equally wide audience. The entire Franciscan communication apparatus allegedly has been rallied to stimulate the novices and their messages and to make every effort to isolate the first generation of seers.

These manoeuvres aroused the resentment of the Bijakovići people, who thwarted their rivals and prohibited their access to Apparition Hill. In order to settle this question and channel the tensions, several Franciscans joined forces with a few lay believers to create an alternative shrine on their own 'turf'. With the capital that had been accumulated by then, the Franciscans took legal action (allegedly on behalf of local villagers who fronted for them) to get the Titovac back under the control of the original owners who still dwelled at the foot of the mountain. A bribe here and there did a world of good. Little more than a year later (1984), the old owners had their mountain back. But the star, the symbol of the secular ruler, had to disappear as well. That was one more thing money could do. In the end, the cross was restored to its old glory.

But the mountain also had to intrigue people and induce them to come to it, and in this connection, a sacralization process was put into motion. (I was able to experience various of its components first-hand in Medjugorje from 1985 through 1990, though not a word was said about it in Bijakovići, where the very idea was dismissed with contempt.) Recurrent themes included the sudden appearance and equally sudden disappearance of large fires on the mountain, brightly shining balls that were attracted by the cross, healings for people who had watched them intensely, the sun bowing before the cross, sparkling auras, and gleaming figures of the Virgin Mary and Christ. All of these things were said to happen there, though no one actually witnessed anything himself. The propaganda machine worked, as everyone in Bijakovići could attest. 'It is not Apparition Hill, but it definitely is special. I ought to go there one of these days'. This was the kind of comment I could hear the pilgrims make in those days.

It was not long before the Križevac became a popular attraction. Ever since 1985, every day a group of pilgrims has gone to the mountaintop, where an outdoor Mass is held, and the Virgin Mary is said to convey her messages. Miraculous healings take place there, and once a week a nocturnal torchlight procession is organized to the Križevac. There is also ample material evidence that this is a flourishing religious enterprise. Homes had been converted into boarding houses and shops and stalls selling food, sweets and devotional objects now line the foot of the Križevac. Sidewalk cafes and restaurants have sprung up, there are two taxi stands and there is even a photographer to immortalize whatever pilgrims might be interested in side-by-side with a cardboard seer.

Medjugorje and Bijakovići keep careful watch on each other. Each and every manoeuvre one of them makes is soon countered by the other. As soon as 'the competition' offers a better buy, prices are adjusted according-ly. One of the effects of all this is that the two centres have come to look more and more alike. This is presumably another reason why, as far as I know, the pilgrims have never been that interested in the fact that the two mountains had such totally different backgrounds. Both of them are sacred places where God's special grace is revealed every day via the Vir-gin Mary and her helpers, the seers. As Stirrat (1984) put it, pilgrims have a mythical or cosmological approach rather than a historical one. For the local villagers, with a far more historical awareness in this respect, the differences are all the greater. The people of Bijakovići view their moun-tain, Apparition Hill, as the only real one. In Medjugorje, however, much more emphasis is put on the economic miracle that the Mother of Jesus bestowed. The two parties do agree on one point: both fear Gromovnik's fiery breath. For despite modern techniques, fires still spontaneously break out. Fire prevention is no longer backed by collective rituals; at most a certain extent of attention is still devoted to it in the home. But representations can sometimes be very stubborn, which is perhaps another reason why especially the older people are still apt to refer to the moun-tain as Grmljavinac.

Conclusions

This chapter described a complicated political process, a power struggle focused on the definition and domination of Mount Šipovac. Stages of sacralization alternated with stages of secularization in a relatively fixed pattern. The establishment of a new secular rule implied secularization: the dominating religious regime was relegated to the background, the mountain was closed off and pronounced military terrain. But to make a regular control over the peasant population feasible, coalitions were ente-red into with religious leaders for varying lengths of time, thus once again setting in motion a process of sacralization as regards Mount Šipovac.

The course of the power struggle that went on for centuries and the development of the mountain's signification constitute a function of the religious and political integration of the local community into larger social frameworks. Initially a sacrificial site for quasi-autonomous local clans and only periodically visited by a few of the clan elders to appease a pantheis-tic god, the Šipovac changed into a Christian place of reconciliation of a parochial nature, and was then transformed into a widely visited international sacral 'power station'. Growing numbers of people became more and more directly involved in a sacralization process, which exhibited a clear tendency toward monopolization. But this development unintentionally generated a counter-movement in the sacral centre itself. As a result of the huge expansion of the devotional centre, growing numbers of people became increasingly involved in providing material services for pilgrims. This took place at the expense of their direct commitment to the sacral aspect. In other words, a process of relative secularization took place among the local population, a process evident at other devotional centres as well (cf. McKevitt 1988, Vissers 1989, Sallnow 1991, Kselman 1978). A development of this kind can expand far beyond the sacral centre and can even influence the entire devotional regime. Various pilgrimage sites and devotional movements linked to them have thus fallen into obscurity or total decay (cf. Crumrine and Morrins 1990, Zimdars-Swartz 1991). Religious specialists have been known to try to alleviate an insidious development of this kind by bringing the tasks related to accommodating pilgrims under their own direct supervision. Their virtually total monopoly over the accommodations at Lourdes, Fatima, and Guadaloupe are good examples.

Since the war broke out in Bosnia Hercegovina, there have been indications of the sacral centre of Medjugorje shifting meaning once again. With the declining international pilgrimage and the rapidly increasing numbers of Croat soldiers and Croat (political) refugees returning from abroad, Medjugorje has become—now more openly—a centre of national Croat identity and community. Šahovnicas (Croat national emblem) painted on houses and rocks, on signposts and shields of Križevac and Apparition Hill; black busts of Tudjman and swastikas, together with white statues of the Virgin Mary exposed in the tourist shops; loudspeakers in cafes and private houses and on Križevac alternatingly producing religious hymns and old once-forbidden Croat songs: all this seems to testify that Mary supports the Croat cause and that Medjugorje has entered a new stage in the (differential) sacralization process.

Notes to Chapter Six

1. Cf. Goudsblom (1988: 2), who noted that there is not really any counterconcept to secularization. That author feels this is related to the dominant view that people 'have actually always been religious', a view Douglas (1982) also referred to with more than a hint of scepticism.

2. More details of this ritual complex will be given in Chapter Seven.

3. I was not to have access to any detailed information about the ethnic conflicts at the time until the summer of 1991. It had been kept 'secret' and as I realize in retrospect, my informants had always managed to steer my questions in some other direction. This sudden openness had to do with the ethnically based battle already raging in full force in Croatia and on the verge of breaking out in my research region as well.

4. The Hapsburg ruler had never ordered an actual military occupation of the mountain, nor had the mountain ever been transferred to the Franciscans, as there was widespread distrust of these nationalistic, militant leaders. But when Serb opponents wanted to set up a religious 'outpost' there, the secular authorities intervened and for the time being, the mountain was off-limits for everyone.

5. I do not know of any Serb or Chetnik reaction to this Catholic countermove.

6. No one knows the exact figures, but the estimates for all of the Croatian State vary from 200,000 to anywhere from 800,000 to 900,000.

7. When I came in the late summer of 1991 and went to this open cemetery with only a simple commemorative plaque, bullets whizzed past me into the wood. My informant, who had put on a disguise for the occasion, had warned me that groups of armed men had been sighted at various historical places in the region. Creeping like tigers, we were able to leave the field of fire of the *Četnići*, which is what my informant felt sure they were. More about this ominous place will be given in the Epilogue.

8. See Chapter Eight.

9. The vendetta or blood feud is a way of administering justice between two or more groups of blood relatives (tribes or clans), whereby a member of one group has the right and obligation to kill a member of another group to avenge some injustice that has been done. The group that has thus lost one of its members, i.e. that has 'lost blood', then has the right and indeed obligation to take blood, i.e. to take a life, from the first group. In principle the vendetta is an unending process that can escalate to take any number of human lives. The vendetta does not take place within a group of blood relatives. That would be contrary to cultural logic, since it would mean taking blood of one's own group, so that one would end up with a double loss. Conflicts within the group are always settled in some other manner. A cycle of violence is usually terminated when—under the supervision of a clergyman and the clan elders—the parties engage in lengthy negotiations and finally arrive at some agreement. These negotiations were always held in secret, although the actual 'sealing' of the agreement was a public celebration where goods, food, drinks and arms were usually exchanged.

Chapter Seven

Gomila's Saints: Ritual and Violence Control

'The evolution of a ritual complex illustrates at an intimate level the dynamics of power relations.'
(Raymond Firth 1981)

It was a cloudy Sunday morning early in June 1990. At the church of Saint James, the local patron saint, the bells were calling pilgrims to attend mass, to venerate the Blessed Virgin Mary and to receive her special messages via the seers. At the same moment, though probably unnoticed by any of the pilgrims, another group of people was moving toward the outskirts of Gomila, a hamlet of Bijakovići. On that particular Sunday morning, some six hundred villagers were hurrying to the Gomila cemetery, a site in the wilderness virtually concealed from sight by boulders, shrubs and trees and solely linked to the outside world by a narrow path.

The people of Gomila gather there at regular intervals for what they call a *slava*[1], a ritual complex consisting of two components. One component is focused on their *sveći* (saints), as the founders of their respective *familije* (clans) are referred to. They venerate these ancestors and ask them for favours, protection and the preservation of the peace. The other component is virtually identical to a Roman Catholic eucharist and, depending on the circumstances, can include a baptism, wedding or funeral ceremony. Gomila consists of three patrilinear, patrilocal, exogamous clans linked to each other by marriage, affinity and godparenthood. The Jerkovići are the oldest, most respected clan. They were the first to settle in Gomila (around 1250) and have the best vineyards and tobacco fields (Vego 1981). Their position is also evident at the cemetery, where they have the front row of graves, which are the most beautiful and the largest. The Šivrići occupy the second place on the social and economic ladder as well as at the graveyard. The Ostojići come last: they were the last to settle in Gomila, where their fields are less fertile and their graves are in the last row.

In their Sunday attire, with the men separate from the women and young children, they came to the cemetery that Sunday morning in June to have their fields and their clans blessed. Under the watchful eye of Djure Gorac, a Franciscan priest from the parish, all the heads of the families deposited tobacco, grape leaves and other fruits of their land on a special roofed niche in the large grave of the clan founders. Then the women followed suit. At the grave of their own clan forefather, they placed objects belonging to relatives who were in poor health or had ill fortune of some other kind, in the hope that via the objects, they could convey new strength to their homes. The oldest men of each clan, the *starešine*, formed a guard of honour around the grave of their clan founder and the other men stood at the graves of their closest relative. The women and the children then formed one large circle, hand in hand, around the three rows of graves. Now Father Djure stepped forward, he stood across from the oldest of the Jerkovići and intoned a hymn. After the first line, the men joined in. Resonantly and in harmony, they thanked their clan founder for their prosperity and asked for his unending protection and assistance. Then the other two clans repeated the same ritual. The session closed with the high, monotonic a cappella singing of the women. The prevailing theme in their 'litany' was peace and unity among the clans. Then several of the elderly clan members gathered all the objects from the graves in a huge wooden bowl. Ceremoniously accompanied by Father Djure holding a large candelabrum with three candles, they carried the bowl to the cemetery chapel. Under the watchful eye of the statues of Saint James and the three clan founders, the bowl was placed before the altar. The ritual closed with a speech and a short eucharist. Then everyone went home to exchange food and special delicacies with their relatives and godfathers.

A considerable part of this ritual is very old. It dates back as far as 1523, when a monk by the name of Miho wrote a lengthy account of it, which is quoted in its entirety in Vego's historical work on the Brotnjo region (Vego 1981).

This chapter describes the origin and evolution of that ritual complex in Gomila. War, blood vengeance and power politics within and between religious and secular formations are important conditioning forces.

Turkish Violence and the Formation of a Ritual Complex
(1470-1878)

In the course of the fourteenth and fifteenth centuries, the Turks conquered large parts of what is now ex-Yugoslavia. The western region of Bosnia Hercegovina, mainly populated at the time by Catholic and Bogumil Croats, became one of the northern outposts of the powerful Ottoman Empire (Knežević 1961).

In the Brotnjo, like elsewhere, the delicate equilibrium of the feudal system was disturbed. The three aristocratic families who ruled Brotnjo were banished or murdered and their possessions were divided by the sultan among three *begs* or *spahis*. These military vassals of the sultan settled with their troops in the town of Čitluk. They abolished the old feudal system and forced the peasants to pay higher taxes than they ever had in the past (Soldo 1964). This rapacious governing style soon led to widespread popular opposition. Small gangs of *hajdući* or *ustaši* were formed, who attacked tax collectors, ambushed trade caravans and obstructed the new rulers in whatever ways they could (Koljević 1980; Balić 1991).[2] These gangs hid out in the inaccessible regions of Hercegovina, and in the winter they stayed with relatives or took refuge in nearby Montenegro, where they joined with ferocious groups of warriors who were never ruled for long by the Turks. Together they regularly set forth on marauding expeditions (Koljević 1980; Boehm 1985). The Turks responded with bloody reprisals. The *hajdući* and their immediate relatives were taken by surprise in their homes, beheaded on the spot or impaled alive on spikes. If they failed to apprehend the gang members immediately, the Turks would organize a communal hunt. If they still could not be found, randomly selected villagers would be tortured until they named the members of the gang or revealed their secret hiding place (Koljević 1980; Balić 1991; Vego 1981). Forcing people to betray each other this way led to a dramatic revival of blood revenge (*krvna osveta*). The successful efforts made during the feudal rule of the region to minimize these vendettas and reduce their significance were now undone (Soldo 1964).

Spahi Osmok was the first Turkish ruler in Brotnjo to try to pacify his domain (Vego 1981). The realm under his control covered the entire northern section of Brotnjo, including Gomila. To avenge the murder of his daughter by *hajdući* from Gomila, his predecessor had massacred virtually all the members of one of the three clans, only to then be slaughtered himself. Osmok made no effort to avenge this murder, but chose instead to bury the hatchet. He allowed a group of Serb refugees from the south to settle in the vacant and largely devastated hamlet, which was now called Ostojići after the founder of the Serb clan of that name. For the period of one year, he granted them partial exemption from paying tribute.

Though these steps did make for a more disciplined mode of rule, they did not reduce the acts of vengeance among the population. The vendettas, which seemed to be self-perpetuating, greatly reduced the productivity of the region (Soldo 1964). In an effort to put an end to the bloodshed, *spahi* Osmok took what might have seemed at the time to be quite an out-of-the-ordinary step. In 1512 he invited a number of Franciscan monks from the monastery of Živogošče on the northern border of Bosnia to settle in his realm. In exchange for the restoration of order and the regular payment of tribute, the priests were promised lodgings, tax exemption and a moderate extent of religious freedom, including the right to engage in missionary activities (Vego 1981).

Upon closer consideration, this step on the part of the Turkish ruler was actually quite a logical one. In the past, Bosnian princes and feudal lords had called upon Franciscans to assist in the domestication and integration of certain segments of the local population. These Order priests, many of whom came from the region, had with virtually no exception been highly skilled at linking economic to religious interests (Fine 1975; Quaestio 1979). As to integrating Christian representations and customs with traditional popular ones, they had exhibited similar virtuosity (Fine 1975; Koljević 1980; Karadžić 1935; Balić 1992). This had repeatedly led to serious clashes with the Holy See, but their multifarious resources had enabled them to keep Rome from replacing them with a firmly established and loyal diocesan organization (Fine 1975). In short, Osmok had found himself a clever and experienced coalition partner, and one that was incessantly at loggerheads with the Ottoman arch-enemy in Rome.

Although sizeable problems faced the Franciscans, they were not easily discouraged. The key to their energetic approach might be referred to in contemporary terminology as ritual and ceremonial integration. The Serb and the Croat communities were both in the habit of gathering at regular intervals to honour the founders of their clans. In the case of the Croat Jerkovići and Šivrići, this was a modest ritual that each clan performed separately at the home of the clan elder and under his supervision (Vego 1981). In Serb circles, however, the worship of the clan founder had traditionally been part of a large-scale communal ritual, the *slava*, which was led by priests of the Serbian Orthodox Church. Hospitality, fraternity and forgiveness were central themes in the ritual.

In their efforts toward integration, one of the Franciscan achievements was that the three clans were permitted to furnish one common site for ritual purposes. They were not allowed to construct a church, but a cemetery with a small chapel did not fall under the Turkish prohibitions. The graveyard was soon to become a centre of ritual activities for Gomila. In addition to the rites and festivities of the separate clans, ceremonies were regularly held there together in honour of their respective ancestors. The Serb *slava* with its prayers, blessings, hymns and meals served as a model. This explains much of the development of the contemporary ritual complex of Gomila, which is a mixture of Serbian Orthodox, traditional local, and Roman Catholic practices (Vego 1981).

The Franciscans were able to further reinforce interclan ties by reintroducing fixed, ritually sanctioned rules pertaining to marriage and godparenthood. In this sense, they were merely following the example of the three families of the feudal lords prior to the Turkish occupation, who had been plagued by similar rivalry, blood feuds and other violent acts of revenge. Each clan was granted a specific, but situationally altering, function vis à vis the other two clans. The rights and obligations of the bride-giving and bride-receiving clans were supervised by the third clan, which also provided the godparents for the children born from the marriage.[3] In this way the Jerkovići, the Šivrići and the Ostojići were interwoven in a highly complex fabric of interpersonal control.[4]

Their success put the Franciscans in a relatively strong bargaining position with *spahi* Osmok. They succeeded in reducing the peasantry's tribute, and acquired a monopoly over its collection. Next to the graveyard, the priests built a fortified storage depot and had it manned by Turkish soldiers. Remains of the depot can still be seen at the Gomila cemetery.

Osmok had made a wise policy decision, and his example was followed by the rulers of other sections of what is now Medjugorje parish. Six cemeteries-cum-chapels were soon in use in this fertile section of the Brotnjo district. They were the first 'parish churches' in the region, because prior to Turkish rule, peasants' spiritual needs were met by travelling groups of monastery-based Franciscans who performed wedding, baptism and funeral ceremonies (Vego 1981; Craig 1988; Quaestio 1979).

In the end, however, all these Franciscan efforts failed to make Brotnjo a permanently pacified part of the Ottoman Empire. On the contrary, in what came to resemble a relatively fixed pattern, periods of internal and external pacification alternated with periods of violence and hostility, and this continued up to the end of Turkish rule in 1878 (Vego 1981; Soldo 1964; Quaestio 1979). This pattern was largely shaped by the competition mechanism dominating relations between the Turkish *spahis* and Franciscan clergy. It was the clergy who made it possible for the Turkish rulers to rely on the relatively regular payment of tribute. The Franciscans in turn made good use of the fruits of their role as intermediaries. They invested their revenues in land, and to an even larger extent in tollage and in trade monopolies on the city markets. With this capital, they managed to acquire even more privileges. This expansion was largely at the expense of the Turkish vassals. They must have been green with envy as they watched the rise of these super-entrepreneurs. But it was only when the tax pressure of their overlord became too great to bear—and due to war economies, this was regularly the case—that they exhibited large-scale active resistance. The clergy were then deprived of their property and exiled. The right to collect taxes was leased to the highest lay bidder, who then went ahead and increased the tribute. This led to widespread opposition on the part of the local people. They were absolutely unwilling to pay a higher tribute; they wanted to pay a lower one, since a part of their payment had hitherto gone to their religious leaders in exchange for services and protection they provided. The refusal to pay tribute was met by armed intervention, which only served to make the opposition of the local population even more fervent. In times like these, the abduction of brides was not uncommon, and this played a role in inciting violence and animosity. This cycle of violence was not broken until the Franciscans once again established themselves there. But this in turn gave rise to a new round of internal and external violence. In short, the Turkish rulers and the Franciscan priests were doomed to each other, and the *slava* was the ritual expression of this destiny.

Hapsburg Centralization and Local Resistance: Christianization of a Ritual (1878-1918)

After the mid-nineteenth century, the Turkish Empire disintegrated. Internal dissension, frequent attacks by Serb and Croat guerillas and external pressure from Russia and the Hapsburg Empire were the main causes. In 1877, Bosnia and Hercegovina shook off the Turkish shackles. But the flush of freedom was to be short, for in 1878 the Congress of Berlin gave Austria-Hungary the mandate over the region, which was completely annexed to the Danube Monarchy a decade later. Numerous unsuccessful rebellions were the result.   In order to maintain effective rule over the area and optimally capitalize on its natural resources, the Hapsburg monarchs introduced a strongly centralist military bureaucratic system. Their goal was Europeanization. They constructed road and railroad networks, instituted a Western system of government and legislation, and stimulated the mining, lumber, tobacco-processing and numerous other industries.

In the field of religion as well, the aim of the Catholic Hapsburgs was to gain maximum control over their new colony. In consultation with Rome, the monarch devised a diocesan system for the region and a division into parishes. All the regular clergy, most of whom were Franciscans, had to make way for secular priests who, like the bishops, were to be nominated by the king and then appointed by Rome. Thus a hierarchic, easily controllable and loyal church apparatus was to be created to take the place of what Rome viewed as an obstinate, unorthodox and intractable network of Franciscans.

On paper, the reorganization was rapidly carried out, but the actual alterations were not that easy to put into effect. Due to lack of secular priests, the opposition of the population and the lack of cooperation—and that is putting it mildly—of the Franciscans, the entire plan ended in a fiasco and the Franciscans remained in control.[5] The Hapsburg church policies had nonetheless caused much unrest, rivalry and tension throughout the area, including Gomila and other parts of the new parish of Medjugorje.

Since there were so few locally-born secular priests, in 1892 the new bishop of Mostar, a Hungarian himself, assigned the organization of the new parish of Medjugorje to Tomaslev, another Hungarian. Tomaslev was assisted by several Slovene secular clergymen. Tomaslev's first task was to build a parish church where the liturgical ceremonies and sacraments could be properly performed. The Hungarian archdiocese was to donate the bulk of the construction costs, and the rest was to be provided by the local population.

In the countryside, newcomers are usually noticed quite quickly. So it could not have been long before the presence of the new priests in Medjugorje led to questions and speculations on the part of the local peasants. Soon the rumour went round that their Franciscan spiritual leaders were to be replaced by foreign priests and that their *slavas* could no longer be performed because the worship of ancestors was not in keeping with the doctrine of Rome. For baptism, wedding and funeral ceremonies, they would now have to go to a church, which was to be built at their expense and on their land. All this must have been extremely upsetting, though the unrest is only indirectly evident from the sources (cf. Vego 1981; Quaestio 1979). The opposition never actually resulted in acts of violence, probably thanks to the placating influence of the Franciscans, but the people had other ways of pestering and boycotting to make their feelings known. The Slovene priests who did the door-to-door collecting for the construction of the new church were chased away without further ado. And despite the attractive opportunity to earn a bit of money, none of the local residents wanted to have anything to do with the construction. Austrians who had settled in the nearby town of Čitluk in keeping with the Hapsburg emigration policy had to be brought in to do the work.

Many stories still circulate among elderly villagers about the four years it took to build the church (1894-1898). The whole construction process was a fiasco: the land that was purchased—which is claimed to have been Franciscan property that was sold via a front-man—was a marsh. As soon as the first wall section was completed, parts of it caved in and collapsed. The people of Gomila felt this was the doing of their ancestors, who disapproved of the church. By giving their ancestors more and more sacrificial offers, they hoped to induce them to commit further acts of revenge. The story is also still going round that construction pastor Tomaslev antagonized several of the village ancestors by having the sacrificial niches on their graves cemented shut. The reprisals were not long in coming: soon the clergyman found all the windows and doors of his hostel in Medjugorje cemented shut. It is said that if you look closely, you can still see signs of this on the hostel. The Austrian construction workers and their families, who lived in huts at the construction site, also had a hard time of it. They had to supply their own building material and tools, since the local population refused to cooperate in any way. The same held true for food and clothing, which had to be brought in from Čitluk. This dramatic factional dispute came to one of its many climaxes just before the church was to be consecrated by the prelate of Mostar. He had ordered a large statue made of Saint James, the new patron saint of the new parish. The statue is said to have come tumbling down from its pedestal the day before its consecration, damaging the altar in the fall. In the opinion of several of my informants, there could have been no clearer proof of ancestral vengeance.

In 1898, after numerous trials and tribulations, the church was finally completed. However, the villagers continued to steer clear of it. According to one of the older informants, it had been the firm conviction of his parents' generation that whoever ventured over the threshold evoked the wrath of the forefathers.

When all the construction work was completed, the Austrians said farewell, leaving the new parish church empty. Not long afterwards, in 1904, the Slovene diocesan priests departed as well. They withdrew 'on their bishop's orders', or so the official diocesan version went, because they had only been lent to the diocese of Mostar for a limited period of time (Quaestio 1979). But the same source notes that a number of former diocesan clergymen exchanged the priest's habit for that of a Franciscan monk. Whatever the case may be, in the first few decades of the twentieth century, the Franciscans were once again masters of this remote corner of the Hapsburg Empire.

The clan forefathers were also rehabilitated and restored to their place of honour, though their hegemony was over. From then on, they had to share their position with Saint James and his sanctuary, the parish church, and the period that followed was one of adjustment and reorganization.

For centuries on end, political circumstances had severly obstructed the maturation of the Roman Catholic Church in Bosnia and Hercegovina. In a number of senses, they had remained missionary regions. There were hardly any churches and the Franciscan missionaries lived in what few monasteries there were. From there they travelled round the area in small groups, and sometimes lodged temporarily in the homes of local peasants. In many cases, their spiritual task was confined to performing baptism, wedding and funeral ceremonies and settling disputes. It was only in those few places where local protection or other factors had enabled them to build a chapel, as was the case in Gomila, that they could perform a wider range of rituals with greater regularity. Throughout the region, however, these rituals mainly consisted of local customs linked to some manner of church ritual; a full-fledged mass with a eucharist was virtually unknown in the countryside here (Quaestio 1979). Under unceasing pressure from Rome, the Franciscans now made every effort to alter this. The regular visitation committees from the Holy See complained about numerous heathen practices, superstitions, and contamination of church services with foreign (i.e. Serbian Orthodox) liturgical elements. References were also repeatedly made to the poor educational level of the Franciscans. In an effort to reduce this pressure from Rome, the Franciscan clergy established several seminaries in their province. Not only were novices trained here in keeping with the new rules, all the Franciscans from the entire region were given periodic training courses and instructions for innovations in their parishes. The implementation of these innovations was not a simple matter and, presumably to help prevent tension and opposition, many traditional elements were incorporated into the new liturgical practices.

It still was not easy for the priests of Medjugorje parish to coax their parishioners across the church threshold. Some older villagers still remember that their fathers absolutely refused to set foot inside that building. As they were nonetheless determined to adopt their policies, the priests had little choice but to resort to tried-and-true strategies. Since they controlled the local school system, they had no trouble 're-educating' younger parishioners via their catechism lessons. They also managed to establish closer bonds of loyalty with local women by organizing them in prayer groups and educating them. The veneration of the Virgin Mary was promoted, particularly among the women. Thus some of the congregation members gradually became familiar with the new liturgical cult. Slowly but surely, these 'trend-setters' encouraged quite a few of the men to share their enthusiasm. And to augment the men's loyalty, a shortened eucharist ceremony was added to the ritual meetings at the chapels of Gomila and the other cemeteries.

By 1920, a 'two-track' religious policy was being implemented in Medjugorje parish. Orthodox ceremonies prescribed by Rome were being promoted, but so were traditional local clan rituals. For the major religious holidays and the veneration of the Virgin Mary, the parish church was the ritual centre, but the traditional local rituals, be it in an adapted version, were still carried out at Gomila and the other five cemeteries-cum-chapels of the parish. However, the relative 'peace' created in this way was not to last long. The violence of war destroyed the fragile equilibrium, soon leading to a vehement outburst of the ever-latent centrifugal forces.

World War II and Guerilla Fighting: The Ancestors Go Underground

After the downfall of the Danube Monarchy, the Kingdom of Serbs, Croats and Slovenes was founded in 1918. As described in Chapter Six, the (Serb) king soon disbanded the Parliament and instituted a veritable reign of terror. All opposition was suppressed and groups of Četnići were free to plunder and loot the Croat villages. The events that ensued were loathsome and vile. In Čapljina, not far from Medjugorje, the Četnići practised their swordsmanship by tossing babies into the air and catching them on the tips of their sword. In another nearby village, they built special houses for hanging rebellious Croats (Maček 1957; Tomasevich

1975; Jelić-Butić 1986). The originally Turkish custom of impaling rebels on spikes was also a common reprisal. These vicious acts of violence soon gave rise to equally vicious *Ustaši* who operated in small guerilla units, thwarting the Serb authorities and retaliating in Serb regions. They later joined forces under Ante Pavelić, already notorious for his savage atrocities, who was mainly to make a name for himself in World War II.

In 1941 the Axis powers invaded Yugoslavia and met with very little resistance as they occupied most of the country. In order to intensify the hostilities between Serbs and Croats and to exploit their dissension, the Germans and Italians founded the Independent State of Croatia. The actual power was in the hands of Pavelić and his *Ustaši*. Their goal was to purify the state of Serb elements, starting in the ethnically mixed region of Bosnia Hercegovina. Serbia fell under the direct administration of the Germans and was ordered to demobilize its army. But the *Četnići*, the former aides of the state police, withdrew as resistance fighters and formed their own guerilla units in remote parts of the country.

In what was Yugoslavia, World War II was very much a civil war among those guerilla groups (Maček 1957; Alexander 1979; Ristić 1966; A. Djilas 1991). To a greater extent than the regular occupying troops, the Serbs and Croats attacked each other's towns and villages, plundering, looting, murdering and carrying out horrendous atrocities. A third party, perhaps more brutal and ferocious than the other two, soon came to play a role in this harrowing civil war: the Partizans led by Tito. With Allied and Russian help, in the course of time this Communist leader managed to gain control and to found the later socialist federal state of Yugoslavia on Bosnian soil. According to many informants, the real tyranny began then.

Bosnia Hercegovina was the major battleground in this complicated war. In the northern parts of the region, most of the battles were fought between the Allied and German armies; hostilities among the guerilla groups mainly took place in the middle and south. The south was also the site of the greatest material damage and human suffering: more than 50% of the homes were destroyed and 60% of the villages were abandoned as the people had either perished or fled (Maček 1957). Medjugorje was among the villages that had paid the heaviest toll.

'One morning in May 1941, I was having breakfast with my sons', Ivan Jerković, 78, told me in 1988, 'when we heard shots. At first we did not pay any special attention; we thought a hunting party was riding by. But when the shooting continued, I went outside to see what was happening. I heard screaming and weeping. I picked up my gun and told my sons to do the same and come with me. I thought maybe there was a bear or a pack of wolves'. But as soon as the three men crossed the street to where the Ostojići lived, they saw that quite a different kind of attack had taken place. The cows, goats and poultry had been slain; the bloody cadavers were all over. The people of the clan were beside themselves with rage. One of them, Rajko, cursed and shouted as he approached the three men. A gang of *Ustaši* was responsible for the raid. Rajko's wife, who had come to work in the cow shed early that morning, had recognized one of them as Anton Šivrić. In 1937, several Šivrići had been attacked by a gang of *Četnići*. A vicious fistfight ensued, resulting in a great deal of material damage for the Šivrići and many wounded among their ranks, including Anton. Shortly afterwards, this young Croat had left for the north, where he reported to *Ustaši* commander Pavelić. The *poglavnik* (leader) sent Anton to Italy for special guerrilla training at a *Ustaša* training camp. On the day in question, he had come with his squad to take revenge on the Ostojić *familija*, who were originally Serbian. For fear of reprisals by the Ostojići, the Šivrići hurried to fetch Father Leonard, the priest of Gomila. Father Leonard urged them to organize a reconciliation *slava* and to give the Ostojići some of their cattle to compensate for their losses. Unfortunately these plans never materialized. On the eve of the conciliation ceremony, Anton and his gang came back and did serious damage to the sacred site of the Ostojići, the grave of their clan founder.

It seemed as if the spectre of ethnic violence had now reawakened in this region as well. The acts of vandalism committed soon afterwards at the shrines of the Croat clans of the Jerkovići and Šivrići would seem to confirm this. Both held the Ostojići responsible. Their suspicions were confirmed by the disappearance of two young clan men, both of whom were reputed to like nothing more than a good fight. Local tensions intensified, but up to the end of 1942 there had never been anything but material damage in Gomila. Then the conflict escalated and came to be of a totally different nature. Incorporated into a wider framework of antagonism that covered virtually the entire district of Medjugorje, it put more and more lives in danger. Ethnic differences were transformed into rapidly expanding and increasing vicious clan feuds. By the close of World War II in 1945, in Gomila alone approximately 20% of the 400 villagers had lost their lives in clan vendettas.

This dramatic revival of the old blood feud after 1942 was caused by the Partizans, who viewed the region as an *Ustaši* stronghold. Several Partizan groups allegedly led by Serbs and Montenegrins used a traditional method to prompt and promote genocide toward their arch-enemies, the *Ustaši*. The method entailed forcing local villagers to rape and murder other residents of their own neighbourhood or region, with the Partizans themselves playing an active role as well. According to various estimates, approximately a quarter of the population of the Brotnjo plateau (a total of 4,500 to 5,000 people) perished in the course of these 'mandatory' acts of vengeance (Craig 1988; Jelić-Butić 1986).

It hardly needs saying that under these conditions, nothing remained of the old joint *slavas*. The Franciscan priests, ritual leaders of these ceremonies, had either fled the region or had been taken prisoner (Čopić 1963; Hory and Broszat 1965). Some time later, their church was demolished by Partizans, who used the rubble for a crossing over the Lukoc River, where the *Ustaši* had blown up the bridge. As in the other hamlets in the vicinity, the Gomila churchyard and chapel were badly damaged. They were dangerous sites. For several women of the Ostojići clan, who came to make a sacrificial offer to their founder, this peaceful intention was to cost them their lives. At the time, the forefathers were *podzemni*, i.e. they had gone underground, as older informants were quick to explain. At irregular intervals, meetings were secretly held by small groups of relatives in the home of the clan elder. These mini-*slavas* also served a function as 'war council'. Only the men could attend the meetings. The women were far too vulnerable, or so it was said, and had to look after the children. According to several of my informants, however, another reason was the women's double loyalty. Women did not 'belong' to the clan of their husband, but to that of their brother and father. In the event of a conflict, this put them in a difficult position and made their husbands vulnerable.

Thus, World War II violence and local blood feuds had turned a ritually integrated community into a shattered society where even the most elementary security and loyalty were undermined.

A New State: Vendettas in Disguise (1945-1981)

The termination of World War II did not improve the situation in any way. On the contrary, many of my informants felt that was when the tyranny came to a peak. The Partizans, who had won the war with help from abroad, introduced a veritable reign of terror. They were determined to forcefully rid the region of whatever 'fascist elements' were still in evidence and to establish their communist rule here as well. Villages were raided, villagers arrested and tortured, quick trials and executions were common practice. About 3,000 *Ustaši* retreated to the inaccessible regions of Bosnia and southwest Hercegovina in small gangs. A number of men from the vicinity of Medjugorje joined these gangs (Petranović 1963). Aided by sympathizers and relatives, they stormed and sacked public buildings, arms depots and food shipments organized by the new government. A twelve-year reign of terror, a network of secret police and the regular help of on-the-spot informers were needed to eliminate the *Ustaša* movement and its local following. What few *Ustaši* were left had little choice but to flee the country.

It seemed as if law and order were thus restored to the region and that the blood feud had become a thing of the past. But appearances can be deceiving, because ever since the sixties there have been regular incidents of private violence and reprisals indicative of the continuing existence of blood feuds, be it concealed from sight. They occurred behind the stage of the rapidly growing bureaucracies of the government and the Communist Party, where some former peasants from the Medjugorje region had also come to play a role. The tragic fate of Branko Jerković is a good example of the kind of thing that happened at the time.[6]

Branko Jerković from Gomila had worked as a *Gastarbeiter* in West Germany for several years and then spent his savings on a second-hand Mercedes. He wanted to use it to start a one-man taxi service in the nearby town of Čitluk. Via a relative of his who knew a prominent party member who was the head of the license department in Čitluk, he would be able to obtain a taxi license. When this man, Jore Pavlović from Medjugorje, was about to write out the license, he suddenly realized that Branko Jerković might very well be the son of the man who had killed his father in 1939 after an argument about a plot of land near the church. He asked around and discovered that his hunch had been right. Pavlović nonetheless wrote out the license and collected the fee for it. But all the while, he was plotting his revenge. He got into contact with his brother Drago, who he had helped get a job on the police force in Miletina. The brothers decided to set a trap for Branko Jerković, after which it would be easy to dispose of him. One day Branko was arrested by Police Constable Drago. A routine check showed that his transport license did not meet with all the requirements. However, the police constable hinted that for a price, the whole matter could quickly be settled. Branko had to bring a certain amount of money to a spot outside of Miletina at a fixed time, and there he would be given the papers he needed. Branko arrived at the appointed time and handed over the money, but Jore Pavlović then proceeded to beat and murder him. Branko was put into his own car, which was pushed off the road into the ravine. Brother Drago had seen to it that a colleague of his (who was paid to do so) had come along. They had been out on patrol together, or so they later told the judge, when they saw a car stagger up the hill like a drunk and then slide off the road and go crashing into the canyon.

Branko Jerković's older brother Cica did not believe this story. In view of the name of one of the police constables involved, he had a suspicion that it was a case of revenge. A bit of private detective work confirmed his suspicions. Cica set the second police constable's house on fire. Via a high party official who owed him a favour, he managed to keep the fire department from coming to put it out. Fearful of further reprisals, the police constable got in touch with his boss—who was not from the region—to bring the case before the court. The details came out, and the two policemen and Jore Pavlović were sentenced to prison. Some time later, Jore was found in his cell with his skull smashed in and a blood-stained car jack next to the body.

Even after the end of the seventies, the spectre of the blood feud—be it often cast in a new mold—was still haunting the vicinity of Medjugorje and the vendettas continued to flare up now and then. It was not the same as in the past, however, because now people often did not have a clear idea where the danger was lurking. And the *slavas* with their reconciliation efforts were truly a thing of the past. From a quarter where it was least expected, a solution emerged.

Messages from the Virgin Mary and the Revival of a Ritual (1981-1985)

After the end of World War II, several Franciscans had returned to the rectory in Medjugorje. With help from outside the parish, they had been able to build a new church, this time on sturdier ground. The building was opened in 1972, but was only frequented by very few of the villagers. Many of the men steered clear of it for fear of government sanctions and forced their wives to do the same. Under communist rule, the opportunities for an active Christian to have any kind of career were virtually non-existent. This drove the priests to perform their sacramental services in secret at the homes of many parishioners.

The position of the Franciscans was relatively weak for still another reason: they were involved in a dispute with the bishop of Mostar. The bone of contention was hegemony over the spiritual care of the parishioners in the diocese—a long-drawn conflict that was described in detail in chapter two. When this dispute was entering a critical stage for the Franciscans, the Virgin Mary allegedly appeared to six children. Three of them were from Gomila and three were from two other hamlets in the vicinity.

The messages and instructions the Virgin Mary daily conveyed to the children were described in detail and distributed all across the globe. Make peace, pray, fast, and confess were the most important recurrent themes (Blais 1985; Laurentin 1984). In addition to these very general messages, the Virgin Mary is also said to have given very specific messages and instructions to the local population. However, the Franciscans painstakingly kept these messages and instructions out of the general pilgrim circuit.[7] Ljudevit Rupčić, the Franciscan who transcribed all the messages from the very beginning, presents a fascinating overview in a book that is unfortunately not easy to get hold of these days (Rupčić 1983).[8] His book illustrates that the Franciscans supported and stimulated the Marian movement from the very start. They had two aims in mind. One, discussed in detail before, was the prevention of further diocesan encapsulation, and the international pilgrim circuit could help them achieve this. The other aim, which is quite relevant here, was internal pacification. Unlike the case in Turkish times, it was no longer possible for them to enter into a coalition with the secular authorities for this purpose.

The first apparitions expressed the unambiguous instruction to the clans to bury the hatchet.[9] Two of the six seers were claimed to be chosen by the Virgin Mary to serve the parish congregation. They received, it is said, a special grace enabling them to heal the ill, whom they visited in their homes on behalf of the Virgin Mary and healed by laying their hands on them. This was perhaps one of the reasons why they were able to attract steadily growing numbers of women and girls to the church, where they set up prayer groups. During these meetings, the seers said they regularly received instructions from the Mother of God, which were translated by their Franciscan advisers. The instructions pertained to the restoration of the old sacred places and the reintroduction of the slavas. According to Father Rupčić, Marijana, one of the seers from Gomila, had a vision of an American relative who promised to donate money to restore the graves and the churchyard in Gomila. Shortly afterwards the man arrived in the village, arranged for a construction permit and purchased the material that was needed. After the authorities in Čitluk openly approved the plans, the men of the village followed suit and set aside their reservations.[10] Almost every evening, a group of peasants from Gomila would be at work, supervised by priests and advised by a couple of old folks who could still remember how everything had been in the old. Working together like this, discussing, consulting, involving emigrated relatives in the project, had an extremely beneficial effect on a community that had been torn asunder for so long. 'Whenever I had some free time I would help with the work', Petar Šivrić said. 'One evening Janko of the Ostojići—who was working on his row in back of me—asked me whether I still knew who were in the graves next to his parents. Without a moment's hesitation, I started drawing in the sand with him (tracing genealogy). Together with a few other people, we found the answer. I suddenly realized I had helped the man who had probably taken revenge on my father's brother. I told him what I had just realized. Weeping, he fell to the ground. Father Jozo came over. We fetched some young tobacco from the fields, which he blessed and then placed on our *hramovi* (small temples of the clan founders). Father Jozo said that the war had made us all blind. After that I said hello to Janko when I saw him, and our wives took the cattle to drink at our well together, because it gives good water'.

Even the authorities in Čitluk endorsed the project by sending material for a fence. After this gesture and the persistent urging of the Virgin Mary via the seers, the other hamlets also started to do their share of the work. In 1985, with official permission, the first large *slava* was once again held at Gomila.[11] Up to very recently, it was the talk of the town, because it was a truly grand festivity, and many a relative came from abroad to attend it.

Shortly after the ceremony, the Virgin Mary appeared for the last time to the two seers of Gomila. Our Lady informed them, it was said, that their task had been completed.

Pilgrimage, Pacification and Ritual Consolidation (1985-1991)

The grand *slava* of 1985 at Gomila was an important turning point, for ever since then, and up to 1991, ceremonies of the kind were held by the people of the hamlet with frequent regularity. Two priests were appointed for the rituals, which were performed at weddings, baptisms, funerals, the joint celebrations of the clan forefathers and the harvest festivities. Virtually every Sunday, a service was held at Gomila. The worship of the ancestors and the holy sacrament of the eucharist were the central elements. The services differed, however, from those in the past in one important way: the public pronouncement that a blood feud had been settled was no longer a part of it. The clergymen and the other informants all agreed that this was no longer necessary, since the vendettas were a thing of the past, and this view was shared by the authorities.[12] The general consensus was that this had to do with the messages from Our Lady and, even more so, with the mass arrival of the pilgrims. One cynic aptly put it at the time as follows: 'We have to behave ... for the guests. If we start fighting ... they stop coming. My wife Dinka used to be a real tiger ... quicker to use her fists than to do any thing else. Nowadays she says the Lord's Prayer three times a day with the guests before meals and she blesses them when they go to sleep. The guests are in charge now ...'

Conclusion

Although violence and ritual are fundamental aspects of human social life, our knowledge of their interrelatedness is still fragmentary (but see Collins 1990; Elias 1982; Girard 1977; Kertzer 1990; Mennell 1989). This probably has to do with the received Christian notion that violence and ritual belong to totally different domains, and should therefore be studied separately.

This chapter has described the genesis and development of a complex of ritual activities, and violence played a prominent role in it. The evolution of that ritual complex reflected a struggle between secular powerholders and factions of religious specialists for control over the local peasantry. Stagnating integration proved to be the outcome. The local clans were not permanently pacified and durably incorporated into larger social formations. A recurrent cycle of violence led to this stagnation. The underlying causes included two interrelated mechanisms: a violence-generating mechanism and a pacifying-but-polarizing mechanism. External violence generated the conditions for inter-clan antagonism, but also perpetuated the dividing lines along which interclan violence manifested itself. It was not until the massive arrival of pilgrims that this cycle was interrupted and the endemic clan violence was terminated. The ritual complex nonetheless continued for another ten years or so, until the recent war broke out.

Why this continuation? Partly this is because the ritual not only served a pacifying function but for the Franciscan priests it had a defensive function as well, focusing on the preservation of their position in the region. As explained before, this position was threatened by the encapsulation politics of their diocesan counterpart. Continuation of the ritual reinforced their link with the local population, and perpetuated the distance to the diocesan leadership. After all, the worship of ancestors is not part of the official church doctrine, and will thus be discredited by Rome. The reactions this evoked among the population have been recounted above. Another reason for the relatively long continuation of the ritual complex has to do with the Franciscans' position of two-sided dependency. They are not only dependent on the parishioners, but on the pilgrims as well, who in turn rely in any number of ways on the parish population. If local clergy were to neglect parishioners, a phenomenon not uncommon at pilgrimage sites (cf. McKevitt 1988; Vissers 1989; Zimdars-Swartz 1991), this could set a process in motion that would undermine the Franciscan power basis. To maintain the delicate equilibrium, continuing attention focused on the needs and desires of the parishioners was needed. The permanent presence of one seer for the sole purpose of serving the needs of the parishioners is significant in this respect.

The pilgrims are absolutely indispensable when it comes to the process of internal pacification. Their permanent presence in such vast numbers up to the recent war forced a 'peaceful' code of conduct upon the parishioners, and this in turn was one of the factors which altered the entire societal structure. Gomila and the other hamlets rapidly transformed from relative 'isolates' to parts of a much larger social system. The network of dependencies became larger and more complicated quite abruptly, making the 'social constraint towards self-constraint' (Elias 1982) stronger and more elaborate than ever before. It is this civilizing or pacifying role of religion that makes it understandable, at least in part, how and why the cycle of endemic clan violence in Gomila and elsewhere in the region came to an end—for a while.

Notes to Chapter Seven

1. According to some authors, the *slava* is originally a Serb ceremony celebrating the birthday of the clan ancestors (Božić 1972; Koljević 1980). Other authors maintain that *slava* includes other feasts and rituals of smaller and larger groups as well (Rheubottom 1976; Lodge 1941; Hammel 1968; Halpern and Halpern 1972). Still others maintain that it concerns a survival from a pre-Christian past, when each clan venerated its own god (Koljević 1980; Drobnjaković 1960).
2. These terms refer to small para-military groups that were first observed in the early days of Turkish rule (cf. A. Djilas 1991).
3. Hammel (1968) and Koljević (1980) also drew attention to this alliance-forming function of godparenthood.
4. This does not mean the vendetta then totally disappeared from Gomila, though it was greatly reduced (cf. Vego 1981; Soldo 1964). What incidents there were of manslaughter were brought before the council of clan elders, who worked together with the clergy to seek a peaceful solution.
5. See Chapter Two.

6. A bit of detective work on the part of one of my informants, a judge from Čitluk, revealed that in the years 1963 to 1980, no fewer than sixty cases involving vendetta victims in the region came before the court. The following case was also brought to my attention by this judge.

7. Filtering and selective publicity are normal under circumstances like these, as Christian (1987) indicated. Christian also noted that a systematic study of filtered and unfiltered messages and visions presents a good picture of the local history and power relations. See also Chapter Three.

8. Almost immediately after it was published, this book was confiscated by the state authorities and its author was sentenced to fifteen years in prison. There are nonetheless a number of copies in circulation. In a revised version published by Rene Laurentin in 1984, the alleged messages and instructions of the Virgin Mary for the local community were not included.

9. The repeated use of the terms *familije, pomirenje* and *medjusobno* prove this point. It is now also clear how the six young seers, who were certainly not very familiar with the language of the church, could have immediately understood these messages. It was not until later, on the instigation of the local clergy, that this message to the local people was 'translated' into more general terms, referring to 'peace among the peoples'.

10. This approval by the authorities is not surprising. The regular burial of the dead, which had not been organized since the war, was promoted at the government expense.

11. For the simple reason that the numerous pilgrims from abroad brought a steady flow of foreign currency into the region, in the past the government had already proved to be more flexible vis à vis the rapidly growing devotion. Now, however, there was also the widespread notion, a high party official in Čitluk told me in 1990, that cooperation led to unity and helped combat crime.

12. From the mid-1980s up to the beginning of the war, no crimes in the nature of personal vengeance or retribution were registered in this region. According to the same source (Judge M. in Čitluk), there was a spectacular fall in the crime rate throughout the region of Medjugorje.

Chapter Eight

Barbarization: Total Local Warfare

'... [w]e do not fully understand ... the conditions under
which a civilizing process moves ... into 'reverse gear'.
(Eric Dunning 1988)
'... [c]ivilized conduct takes a long time to construct but
can be destroyed rather quickly'.
(Stephen Mennell 1989)
'... [i]f in a society dominant trends can be observed
tending in a certain direction, we are always well
advised to look for counter-vailing trends as well ...'
(Johan Goudsblom 1989)

On the early morning of 27 May, 1992, Ljerka Šivrić
saw something horrible in the neighbouring yard of her father's brother
Djure. Three human bodies, the feet tied to a pipe and the hands behind
their backs, were suspended upside down, immersed up to the shoulders
in the partially demolished cistern. Djure and his two grown sons Ante
and Djure had been savagely slain. Two weeks earlier, on the night of 10
May, a similar drama had unfolded in Siro Ostojić's yard. Someone found
Siro's elderly parents there, hanging from the mulberry tree in front of
the house, their throats slit and their hands chopped off. These are only
two of the long list of atrocities that have dominated life in Medjugorje
ever since the autumn of 1991. Before they knew it, the villagers found
themselves caught up in a vicious spiral of violence. At first it was only
their property they were in danger of losing, but soon it was their lives as
well. In early July 1992, when the Croatian army imposed peace upon the
western part of Hercegovina, local violence came to an end. But Medjugorje's *mali rat* (little war), as the villagers called it, had taken its toll.[1] Of
the approximately 3,000 villagers, an estimated 140 had been killed, 60

were missing and approximately 600 had fled, and a number of buildings had been damaged or destroyed.[2]

Whence this barbarization? How is it possible that after a ten-year reign of the Virgin Mary, referred to locally as the Queen of Peace, villagers started slaughtering each other? Norbert Elias noted that questions of this kind may put us on the wrong track: barbarizing processes presuppose civilizing processes. Thus for a better understanding of barbarization, he feels we ought to concentrate on the civilizing process.[3] This is a useful point of departure. From this perspective, the *conditions* for barbarization processes can be clarified. But it is also a limited point of departure, for it does not provide instruments to elucidate the structure and dynamics of these processes.

This chapter explores barbarization as a relatively autonomous process that, in an academic sense, is of the same ilk as the civilizing process and should be studied along with it.

Civilization: Genesis of a Fragile Veneer

'Here the knife does not go blunt and the (rifle) barrel does not rust', or so an old man concluded his historical view of the region. The recent violence did not surprise him, for it was part of an old tradition of warfare and revenge.

To a certain extent, this long tradition of violence has to do with geopolitical circumstances. Until recently, large parts of ex-Yugoslavia were virtually without interruption border regions disputed by powerful kingdoms and other political power blocs.[4] For almost five hundred years, far into the nineteenth century, the territory was a pawn in the power game between the Austrians and Hungarians to the northwest and the Ottomans to the east. Then it was torn between the Italians and Germans on the Axis side, and the Russians and Allies on the other. And after World War II, up until the end of the Cold War, the capitalist West and the communist East drove a wedge into Yugoslav society (cf. Alexander 1979; Jelavich 1990). These powers not only severely impeded the development of a stable state with effective central control over the means of physical violence, they also created the conditions for growing nationalism and ethnic antagonism (Banać 1984; Cole 1981; A. Djilas 1985, 1991; Ramet 1985; Šimić 1991; Malcolm 1994).

In Bosnia Hercegovina these developments can be traced with the greatest clarity. More than four hundred years of warfare between the

Ottoman and the Hapsburg Empire made the region an ethnic hotch-potch. Large groups of Serbs from the southeast fled to the Bosnian coun-tryside, settling mainly in the less fertile parts (Krajina). Population pres-sure and a sense of adventure led Croats, mainly from the bleak Dalma-tian Mountains, to move southeastward. Large numbers of people eager to take advantage of any opportunity to 'get ahead' converted to Islam, thus laying the foundation for the third ethnic group, the Muslims (Koljević 1980; A. Djilas 1985; Malcolm 1994).[5] During this same period, and in part as a reaction to the frequently harsh Ottoman regime, a tradition of small-scale violent resistance developed in Hercegovina: guerrilla bands of *Had-juci, Ustaši* and *Četnići*.[6] Clusters of these resistance groups made it diffi-cult to permanently pacify the area, and their rivalry promoted acts of revenge and retaliation within and among the various villages (Jelavich 1990; Koljević 1980; Dedijer 1974; Soldo 1964; Vego 1981).

The fall of the Ottoman and Hapsburg empires in 1912 and 1918 did not put an end to these forms of small-scale violence or stop people from taking the law into their own hands. On the contrary, ever since the Kingdom of Serbs, Croats and Slovenes (renamed the Kingdom of Yugo-slavia in 1929) was founded in 1918, they constituted an integral compo-nent—overtly or covertly—of the interaction between the most important groups, the Serbs and Croats (Banać 1984; Ramet 1985).

The prevalent opinion in the region is that Serb and Croat national consciousness goes back to the Middle Ages. At the time, each of the groups was a separate kingdom, parts of which are now disputed territory (Šimić 1991). Foreign rule put an end to their political independence, but religious beliefs (the Serbian Orthodox Church for the Serbs and Catholicism for the Croats) have always remained important identifica-tion and distinguishing factors (Ramet 1984; Rathfelder 1992; Rusinow 1982).

When the Serbs and Croats united to form one independent kingdom, these old distinctions were transformed into rapidly escalating ethnic dif-ferences that soon dominated virtually the entire political arena. Each of the parties was convinced that the other was after hegemonic control. Certainly at the beginning, the Croats had the most grounds for apprehen-sion. The king of the empire was a Serb, the Serbs were by far the largest group; they held almost all the important positions in the government, the bureaucracy, the army and the police force; and every chance they got, they gave their fellow Serbs preferential treatment (A. Djilas 1991). This intensified nationalist feelings, and particularly in the ethnically mixed areas, with Bosnia Hercegovina at the top of the list, tension ran high.

The Serb domination there was characterized by brutal injustice to the Croats, whose political leaders and their local representatives were removed from office and imprisoned. The Croats in turn organized armed gangs called *Ustaši*, who kidnapped Serb leaders and were likely to murder them as well. Neither party had much patience with traitors (Banać 1984; Jelić-Butić 1983; A. Djilas 1991; Čopić 1963; Krizman 1980, 1983; Starčević 1941). Soon this ethnically mixed area, with borders sometimes running through the middle of villages, turned into a 'complex of snake pits joined together by murder, manslaughter, destruction and betrayal' (Soldo 1964).[7]

When the tension spread to other regions and the country became ungovernable, the king disbanded the parliament and instigated a wave of terror. Every trace of opposition was harshly suppressed by gangs of *Četnići*, a loosely organized auxiliary division of the national police, consisting of Serbs who roamed through the Croat areas, robbing and plundering along the way. Their horrendous conduct provoked similar behaviour on the part of the Croats, particularly the Croats of South and West Hercegovina. In this inhospitable region with its coarse and truculent inhabitants, the *Ustaša* groups burgeoned.[8] In tiny guerrilla units, they terrorized Serb communities (Krizman 1980; Jelić-Butić 1986; Tomasevich 1975).

The Second World War deepened the chasm of hatred and magnified the violence to almost unprecedented proportions. With the help of the vicious and pugnacious *Ustaša* organization, the new Independent State of Croatia founded with the support of the Axis powers made every effort to cleanse Croatia, Bosnia and Hercegovina of all Serb elements. The Serbs in these regions sought the help and support of the *Četnići*, who had gone underground *en masse* after the German demobilization of the Yugoslav army. Bosnia Hercegovina turned into a huge battlefield, where guerrillas not only attacked each other, but even more so each other's towns and the civilians residing there, enormous numbers of whom they assaulted, mutilated and murdered in most atrocious ways (Čopić 1963 Anonymous 1986; Jelić 1978; A. Djilas 1991; M. Djilas 1980).

During this period, the *Ustaša* stronghold Medjugorje lost almost half its population. The village also suffered huge material damage, for almost all cattle were slaughtered or stolen and many homes were destroyed, as were crops in the fields.

A third, perhaps even more cruel, party soon joined the war: the Partizans led by Tito. With his dreaded and later renowned guerrilla troops, this communist leader was soon victorious, thanks in part to his incorporation of many *Četnići*, who were being defeated at the time. In 1943, aided by the Allies and the Russians, he founded a new Yugoslav state on Bosnian territory (Parin 1991; M. Djilas 1980, 1983).

A modern (but extremely authoritarian) political, executive and legislative system was built up under Tito, putting a formal end to the ethnic violence and personal feuds. Brotherhood and Unity was the motto of the new order, which was focused on total economic and social modernization along socialist lines. For years, an extremely effective system of repression enabled the authorities to present this fiction—which it certainly was—to the outside world as reality. Although there was a decline in the open hostilities, behind the communist front the old enmity and antagonism lived on undiminished.

Southwestern Hercegovina may have been cleansed of its numerous *Ustaši*, but their relatives were still treated as second-class citizens. They were barred from the ruling communist party and thus could not obtain state benefits and civil service jobs. In all public sectors, the Serbs in the region were in control. As ex-Partizans or their offspring, they dominated the party, public administration, police, army, the bureaucracy and numerous modern government enterprises (Vego 1981). In order to achieve their aims, the Serbs in the region used legal means and methods; the Croats had little choice but to resort to the old forms of self-help. In the formal, legal and political discourse, there were no Croats, there were only 'criminals', 'subversive elements', and 'reactionary forces'. In the hidden discourse of the dominated Croats, however, the opponents were referred to as *Srbi* or *Četnići*. Thus formal rules covertly contributed toward the systematic exclusion of the Croat opponent.[9]

The veneer of the 'new order' gradually began to wear thin. Driven by circumstances, in the early seventies groups of armed young men who called themselves *Ustaši* began to gather in Bosnia and Hercegovina, targeting government institutions, the region's numerous arms depots, party officials, and villages dominated by Serbs (Hofwiler 1992; Gelhard 1992; Soldo n.d.).[10]

In Medjugorje as well, an *Ustaša* cell assembled which, according to my informants, was incorporated in the late seventies into a regional network consisting of several thousand men. In essence this 'organized crime that has spread from the capitalist West', as the regional authorities referred to it, was a reaction to the fact that the Croats had no rights. The response was not long in coming. Particularly in the smaller towns and villages, where the presence of the official authorities was not so keenly felt, vigilantes gathered, which their opponents referred to as *Četnići*. Groups of

Ustaši seemed to be playing a cat-and-mouse game with these *Četnići*, who were sometimes assisted by officials (Soldo n.d.).

Thus another wave of violence began to mount in the region, but this time there was a countervailing trend of a totally different kind. As described in Chapter Two, in 1981 Medjugorje became the centre of a Marian devotional movement focused on peace which rapidly assumed international proportions.

The civilizing influence this pilgrimage centre exerted for almost a decade can be briefly summarized as follows[11]: The mass influx of more than seventeen million pilgrims from all over the world imposed peace-oriented standards of conduct upon the people of the village and entire vicinity. During this period there was a spectacular decline throughout the region in the number of registered crimes, feuds and other forms of violent self-help.[12] The inhabitants of Medjugorje, the region, and indeed the regional authorities benefited from the economic boom resulting from religious tourism.[13]

Barbarization

Eclipse of a Pilgrimage Regime: Rising Tensions

Almost all the villagers renovated their homes to accommodate more pilgrims, enlarging their capital and taking out new loans all the while. Times were good for all of them, although of course they were better for some than for others.

The Ostojići fared by far the best, everyone agreed about that. It had once been a poor clan with very little land, most of which was barren because of its location at the foot of the Mountain of the Cross. This was why so many of the Ostojići had regularly lived and worked abroad, mainly in Germany, the United States and Canada. According to the local population, this had made them a bit strange.

The more signs Medjugorje showed of turning into a flourishing pilgrimage centre, the more Ostojići returned to their native village. With the capital they earned, they soon rose to occupy a dominant position in the religious tourism industry. They built the only two 'real' hotels in the village, and in a neighbouring hamlet built a large bungalow complex for pilgrims, complete with a small chapel. Most of the taxi licences were registered in their name, and at the foot of the Križevac they set up a number of restaurants, outdoor cafes and souvenir shops. They had a monopoly over almost all the bread and alcohol supplied to the village, and ran the most important local branches of national travel agencies. Their influence was not limited to the immediate vicinity. At the most important arrival sites, the airports at Mostar, Split, Dubrovnik and Zagreb, Ostojići agents picked up the pilgrims in Ostojići coaches and brought them to accommodations owned by the Ostojić clan. All these facilities would not have been feasible without an extensive network of connections in the bureaucracies of the district and national government.

Of course this super-entrepreneuring gave rise to jealousy. In particular the Jerkovići and Šivrići, the oldest and most respected clans, felt humiliated by those 'stone-eaters', as they called the Ostojići, whose land was indeed strewn with stones. They themselves had the best land, and there they grew grapes and tobacco. From Vienna to Istanbul, their produce had been renowned for centuries. They looked down on the Ostojići because they were so dependent on *biro četnići*, as they called the (Serb) government officials. A good Croat—and the population of Medjugorje, including the nearby hamlets, consisted of Croats—was independent and took care of business without needing any help. That was the rule they lived by, though they did on occasion have to pay a bribe or two themselves.

As long as everyone was able to profit from the expanding pilgrimage economy, the outbursts of jealousy remained small. But when the impending violence of war gradually cut off this lifeline, matters clearly changed. It started in late summer of 1990. Due to terrorist activities of Serbs and Montenegrins, the southern Croatian coastal regions were unsafe and difficult to reach, which meant a sharp fall in the number of pilgrims. When Croatia declared its independence in December of that year, it only served to intensify this trend. And by early spring of 1991, when Croatia and the federal troops were engaged in open warfare, most of the boarding houses in Medjugorje had barely had a paying guest for some time. Thanks to bribes and good connections, only the ones owned by the Ostojići were still partly occupied. Virtually all the villagers had gone deeply into debt, and when they were hit by hard times, they could no longer tolerate the 'unfair' situation. Leaders of other clans began to negotiate with the Ostojići about dividing 'what little there was'. The negotiations, it is said, did not proceed smoothly. On the contrary, a lot of old resentment surfaced, and in the end the Ostojići refused to share their favourable entrepreneuring position with anyone. The story goes that the parties did not part in friendship, and in fact Medjugorje's little war was already looming.

Križevac Closed off: End of Pilgrimage

On 15 August 1991, the Feast of the Assumption of the Holy Virgin, two groups faced each other at the access road to the Križevac. A few dozen armed and masked men kept a good three hundred pilgrims, guests of the Ostojići, from carrying out their plan to climb the Mountain of the Cross in prayer. The pilgrims were ordered to leave, which they did after several warning shots were fired in the air. Later that day, accompanied by several Ostojići and a local clergyman, they made a second effort. Again it was in vain. Following the advice of some priests, the pilgrims abandoned their efforts. But this was not the end of it for the Ostojići. They felt they had been humiliated and their rights had been violated, for the mountain was free territory open to everyone. Behind the masks, they had recognized the faces of a number of villagers, who they then reported to the police at the district capital of Čitluk. A police raid a few days later yanked several men from their beds, all members of the Jerković clan.

The Jerkovići were quick to express their great indignation and contempt. In Croat communities in this part of Hercegovina, it was considered cowardly to solve a conflict by summoning police. The police department is an alien power apparatus, and what is more it was up to 1992 staffed by Serbs, the sworn enemies of the Croats (Soldo n.d.). By calling in the police, the Ostojići had proved to be friends of the enemy, 'little Serbs' as one informant put it.

A few days later, two policemen were attacked and beaten in their homes in Čitluk.[14] And in the following week, in one night all thirty-two of the Ostojići taxis were wrecked. The Čitluk police, summoned once again, did not arrive in time to catch the perpetrators; approximately forty men of the Jerković and Šivrić clans had disappeared from the village.

Gangs, Vigilantes, and Ethnic Stigmatization

By now the war in Croatia had drastically expanded and its repercussions were increasingly felt in Bosnia Hercegovina. The Serb communities received arms from Serbia to be able to defend themselves against 'the fascist aggression of the *Ustaša*', as it was called (Glenny 1992). In response, the Croat inhabitants of Bosnia Hercegovina felt threatened and large numbers of them broke into the numerous local munitions and arms depots of the Territorial Defence, which was soon dismantled as a result. In no time, all of Bosnia Hercegovina had turned into a vast constellation of heavily armed settlements (Rathfelder 1992). Side by side with these local vigilantes, small mobile armed units developed of Serbs and Croats, who roamed the countryside independently or in larger groups, causing trouble wherever they went and burglarizing the army's numerous munitions depots. These units, often referred to as *režervisti*, consisted of deserters from the Croatian front, men evading mobilization, members of secret para-military organizations of either Croats (*Ustaši*) or Serbs (*Četnići*), villagers who lost their jobs in the now defunct tourist industry and were on the lookout for loot, and lastly, as in Medjugorje, people running away from the police (Hofwiler 1992). In addition, the various sections of the former Yugoslav army, now divided along ethnic lines, also belonged to this extremely dynamic and complex figuration of attack and defence units, sometimes collaborating with each other and sometimes fiercely battling. 'Armies' of Serbs, Croats or Muslims, who barely differed in any way from the *režervisti* described above, operated in the various regions of Bosnia Hercegovina. Each group tried to gain control over its own patch of the ethnic quilt.

In Medjugorje, the Ostojići feared the rapid disintegration of official authority. These people, whose conduct, ideas and conceptions were so deviant in the region, were regularly identified with the Serb arch-enemy, and were in danger of becoming the victims of a 'cleansing' (*rasčistiti teren*). In this predominantly Croat area, it was not easy to defend oneself against this kind of campaign with the help of one's 'own' *režervisti*; self-defence and the help of the police were needed.

In September 1991, the Šivrići claimed to have observed some changes in the Ostojići hamlet at the foot of the Mountain of the Cross. Every day a small police patrol from Čitluk would come by. The police officers would inspect the streets and fields of the hamlet and then withdraw to the dining room of one of the boarding houses. The men of the Ostojić clan were rarely observed outdoors, and it seemed as if the community solely consisted of women and children. But in the darkness of the homes and late at night on the edge of the Križevac, behind bushes and trees, attentive observers regularly noticed men with guns. Judging from their numbers, they were not just Ostojići men, and further probing revealed that some of them were men no one in the district had ever seen before. It was later concluded from the licence plates on their cars that they were Ostojići in-laws from a town across the Neretva River that was known as a non-Croat town.

On the adjacent home grounds of the Šivrići, these developments were observed with suspicion. It was becoming clear that the Ostojići maintained ties with the *Četnići* and thus belonged to the enemy camp. Tension rose to a peak when one of their boys, said to have been working on a chimney, was shot at twice from the direction of the Ostojići. It gave him such a scare that he lost his balance, fell off the roof and broke his arm.

The next night explosions were heard from the direction of the church-yard, and on the following morning Čitluk police found all the Ostojići graves blown up. The meaning of this act was immediately apparent to everyone: a denial of the rights of the Ostojići in the community and the destruction of their historical roots. In the past twelve months, this age-old custom had been regularly revived on a large scale by Serbs and Croats in the neighbouring extremely militant Krajina region, and it was always the start of a 'cleansing' (Reissmüller 1992; Rathfelder 1992).

After this act of open aggression, things quieted down. But it was a menacing kind of silence, and the Jerkovići and Šivrići were waiting to see how their opponent would respond.

Stronghold Formation, Cleansing and Resistance

Together with men who had left and were now returning, equipped with ample arms, munitions and explosives from the depot in Čapljina, the Šivrići and Jerkovići prepared to 'settle matters once and for all' with the enemy. They made good use of know-how acquired in the army and the Territorial Defence. In Čapljina, some of them had joined the notori-ous Croatian HOS militia.[15] Stepan Jerković, a former army officer, became their leader and the troops were called *Stepanovći* (Stepan's men). Stepan, usually called Stjipe, was backed by six sub-group leaders (*časnići*), who each had a number of men (*vojnići*) under their command.

The first thing they did was barricade the access road at the mountain pass to the plateau where Medjugorje is situated. Day and night, they would hide there and guard the road. This made it impossible for the enemy to receive sizeable reinforcements. Limited help could arrive via mountain paths, but regular patrols were on duty.

It was not only outwardly that Medjugorje began to resemble a strong-hold, but inwardly as well. All the windows in the homes of the clans were blacked out, and wherever possible the lanes were hidden from sight by lines hung with tobacco leaves, branches or straw mats. Virtually undetected by the enemy, it was thus possible to reach each other's prop-erty and gather in groups inside the walled courtyards.

The Ostojići were taken completely unawares by the swift transform-ation into what resembled a fortress. And when they too wanted to make a safe place, they found themselves in the line of fire, though none of the shots hit the mark. Some of the women and children fled to the Križevac, where they were guarded by clansmen hidden from sight. It was only at night, protected by darkness, that they sometimes ventured to return home for their clothes and something to eat or drink. But the enemy was on guard, and responded to their every move with gunfire.

In November 1991, the *Stepanovći* launched their offensive. Their aim was to destroy the cisterns at Ostojići homes. In only a few nights, they managed to blow up 36 of almost 170 cisterns, or at any rate render them useless. Thirty-six families and their livestock had to get water elsewhere. From their hiding places, almost every day the *Stepanovći* managed to shoot a few cattle on the paths.

Fear was mushrooming in the Ostojići camp, for it was evident that a stronger opponent was engaged in a 'cleansing'. One night early in December, there was a skirmish between several of the guards and a few Ostojići. After a fracas, the men managed to break away. It was clear to the *Stepanovći* that they had gone to fetch reinforcements, and so the former intensified their guard patrols.

To this day, Stepan's men do not know how their opponents managed to bring in forty men (the size of two para-military units) without their noticing anything. They were soon confronted with these reinforcements —Ostojići relatives from a village to the south that had been 'cleansed' by Serb militiamen. It was a ferocious confrontation. Firing their rifles as a diversionary measure, the Ostojići succeeded in destroying twelve Šivrići cisterns. This made a large segment of the Šivrić clan vulnerable and dependent upon others.

By Christmas 1991, Medjugorje's little war took a virtually inevitable turn. On the name day of his deceased wife, Mate Jerković, one of the Jerković clan elders, went to her grave to honour her with dried flowers and wild fruit. Mate had trouble walking, which was why he went by mule. As he was passing the ravaged graves of the Ostojići a bullet hit him in the thigh. The bullet was aimed at the mule and not at a person, or so the Ostojići later informed me when I spoke to them in their hiding place. But the flow of human blood had awakened the spirit of revenge.

Mutual Destruction

Blood revenge as a form of self-help is an old and still fairly widespread institution in this part of ex-Yugoslavia. In addition to the state, it was mainly the clergy who—by way of reconciliation rituals—made every effort to attenuate this way of eliminating one's opponents. But in the course of 1991 state power crumbled and the clergymen of Medjugorje were 'summoned back' to their monasteries in Humac and Mostar. This left the parties to their own devices, abandoned to the dynamics of the devastating process they formed with each other. Once it had been set in motion, the process exhibited a tendency toward escalation, driven as it was by the principle of retribution.

Shortly after the start of the new year, this was demonstrated for all to see. Mate's eldest son, the avenger, had shot one of the Ostojići clan elders in the thigh. But when Mate fell ill and died of his wound, his own clan's elders all agreed the retribution had to be taken one step further; Jure Ostojić, a brother of the clan elder shot in the thigh, was shot in the lower back and paralysed for life. His clan refused to accept this and took double revenge: two young Šivrić men were shot in the back, and died on the day of the Feast of the Epiphany (6 January). Obviously this bloodshed put the parties on guard, for since then neither of the clans, at any rate their male members, dared to show their faces much on the streets in the daytime.

Together with a good two hundred other men, most of whom were from the Jerković and Šivrić clans, the *Stepanovći* kept the area closed off. This put the Ostojići and their relatives from outside the area in a perilous position. Their ammunition and food were running out, but if they made a mass break for it, it would probably mean a massacre of their people. Waiting longer, however, would only force them to surrender in the end and leave Medjugorje forever.

For a couple of weeks, nothing special happened; the tension rose and everyone seemed to be waiting for an explosion of violence. It came from an unexpected quarter. Late one afternoon at the end of January 1991, a few military aeroplanes from the base in Mostar flew low over Medjugorje. It later turned out that they were looking for a group of Montenegrin soldiers who had deserted in East Slavonia and were now headed home, plundering as they went (*Mostarski list*, 25 January 1992). Above Medjugorje, the planes (with Serb pilots) began to shoot at the church steeples. They missed, but they did hit a few Šivrići homes. The incident distracted attention from the dominant clans, and the Ostojići were quick to take advantage. Together with some women and children, a group of men managed to reach the pass. Once they got there, however, they met up with the guards. Fierce fighting ensued, and the unprotected Ostojići were clearly at a disadvantage. Quite a few men, women and children were killed; others managed to escape. Some guards also perished in the fighting. In the next few days, each of the parties saw to its dead.

Things were quiet again in Medjugorje, so quiet that a group of unsuspecting pilgrims could move about freely for several days in the Marian Peace Centre.[16] At regular intervals they saw groups of people, mainly women and children, leave the village with their luggage. When asked about it, they said they were fleeing 'the war'. The pilgrims did not witness the movement in the other direction, the armed men entering the village in the dead of night. They were the relatives of the battling clans who had come to the village from 'liberated' areas, men who were no longer needed at home because their villages had been cleansed, and who had sworn to avenge their dead kin.[17]

Denouement

The exodus continued until the end of March. Growing numbers of women and children left, and Medjugorje increasingly became a stronghold of armed men.[18] A small incident sparked off enormous repercussions. At a courtyard of the Ostojići, a few intoxicated men were showing off their skills as marksmen by shooting tins and bottles off a wall with their little scorpion automatic pistols. One of them recklessly tried it with a grenade launcher. The grenade exploded and blew a big hole in the wall of Ante Šivrić's stable a bit further down the street. The shot was immediately answered in kind, and mortar shells soon set two homes ablaze, killing the elderly tenants.

Hardly a day went by without each of the sides doing some damage to the other's property, especially their livestock, supply sheds and cisterns. But it was the sharply rising number of avengers inside the gates of Medjugorje that gave 'the war' another turn: personal retribution in the dead of night or at dawn with a knife and a rope. An estimated eighty people, almost sixty of whom were locals, lost their lives this way; their mutilated bodies, usually hanging from a tree or ceiling beam, bore witness to the atrocious acts.[19]

The complicated process of retribution went on until the end of May, when the denouement came just as suddenly as the start. It was linked to military developments in Bosnia Hercegovina at large. Flanked by irregular militia, a unit of the Croatian army was on its way from Čapljina to Listica. There a Serb military unit that wanted to force a passageway through to the west was being obstructed by armed groups of *Ustaši* from the region. The Croatian troops stopped near Medjugorje for the night.

When patrols found out about what was going on there, a HOS unit from Čapljina decided to go off and rescue their 'Croat friends'. It was a short surprise attack that resulted, as informants later related, in a complete 'cleansing' of the Ostojić hamlet. Well nigh a hundred people, mostly men, were captured and taken off to a ravine in the vicinity, or so the story goes, where they were shot and killed.[20]

At the end of June 1992, I was able to see for myself that Medjugorje was once again accessible for pilgrims. From the coast up to approximately thirty kilometres past the pilgrimage centre, the area had been 'purged' of the 'Serb aggressor'. The area had 'the protection of the Croatian army and its allies', as pamphlets at the customs office announced. The hustle and bustle had returned to the devotion centre. Several hundred pilgrims from Italy, Canada and the United States were being catered to by villagers, who apologized for the inconvenience and the disarray 'the war' had caused. The pilgrims were very understanding, and they were glad that 'these people could live in freedom again' and that 'the Message of Peace had triumphed'. Once again houses were being built and repaired throughout the vicinity, but it did not seem out of the ordinary to the pilgrims, since construction work had been a familiar sight for years. Singing resounded from the Mountain of the Cross: groups of pilgrims were praying the stations. Work was also being done on the private homes in the Ostojići hamlet—by Jerkovići and Šivrići and their relatives who had come to join them. At the cemetery of Medjugorje, concealed behind bushes and trees, part of the ground was left fallow. Only a year earlier, this had been consecrated earth, the last resting place of a clan that was part of this district. Now not a single trace of their existence was left. But somewhere out there, the people of Medjugorje knew, a hatred smouldered that would one day be sparked into flame again.

Conclusion

A discontinuous state monopoly on organized violence, a limited pacification of state territory, and a long tradition of feuding and other forms of self-help might indeed have been the major preconditions for the barbarization process in Medjugorje, but they do not explain the dynamics of the process itself. Elias felt the dynamics of what he called 'cycles of violence' had to do with 'double-bind processes ... which trap [constituent] groups in a position of mutual fear and distrust, each group assuming as a matter of course that its members might be harmed or even killed by another group if the latter had the opportunity and the means to do it'. He went on to note that a figuration of this kind is usually characterized by a 'strong self-escalating impetus' (Elias, in Elias and Dunning 1986: 26). This definition does not seem to be all that applicable to the course of events or the developmental structure of the violence process in Medjugorje. Perhaps a better explanation can be sought in the principle formulated by Goudsblom, albeit in a different context, of 'paired increases in control and dependency' (1989: 21ff). It can be phrased as follows: the parties strive to dominate each other, but as a consequence they unintentionally become increasingly dependent on each other. The Šivrići and Ostojići each tried to reinforce their position and made every effort to recruit outside help to do so. As a result, the violence figuration they formed together expanded, the violence interdependencies extended, and the escalation potential increased. Nonetheless, the duration of the actual escalations was short, and they were more like (external) incidents that were quickly hushed up (cf. also Collins 1990). The course of the process described here has something paradoxical about it: more and more of the actual acts were increasingly 'barbaric' and cruel, but at the same time there was less and less 'spontaneity' and a relatively greater 'control' or 'regulation' of the conduct toward each other. This would also seem to be in keeping with the principle of 'paired increases in control and dependency' referred to above. More and more people imposed more and more pressure upon each other and upon themselves to engage in harsh forms of revenge, but the menacing effect of this also had a deterrent effect and served to inhibit a spontaneous implementation—a striking similarity to the Cold War, a theme Elias (1987) wrote about at great length, though according to Benthem van den Bergh (1989) in a rather one-sided manner.

A question now arises that might in the first instance seem quite absurd: Can the process described here indeed be characterized as barbarization? Speaking colloquially, of course it can. But in sociological terms of Elias' civilizing process, in which increasing control and regulation of behaviour are important features of 'civilization', it seems far more difficult to give a simple answer to this question. A certain extent of ambiguity has been noted in this theory by other authors (e.g. Dunning 1988; Mennell 1989; Goudsblom 1989; Spier 1993), but the proposed alterations mainly illustrate the complexity of the academic question. Civilization and barbarization would seem to be such closely linked or interwoven aspects of processes that it is difficult to stipulate where one stops and the other starts. If we are to adequately describe and explain this interrelatedness, a theory is required that focuses on these close links.

Notes to Chapter Eight

1. *Mali rat* is the term used in the region for small, often local violent operations of the kind traditionally endemic to the area: complicated blood revenge, whereby some-times whole families are killed or driven away, and surprise attacks or pillaging raids on neighbouring villages by roaming gangs of armed men or other relatively small and informal violent groups. According to my informants, *mali rat* can be a side-effect of organized warfare on a larger scale, but it is not equivalent to it. The Second World War and the recent hostilities in Croatia between sections of the former federal army gave rise to numerous eruptions of local violence in Bosnia Hercegovina. When the 'large' war broke out between the 'real' armies at Sarajevo and other cities in April 1992, it re-activated these local feuds. The small-scale local wars have become closely interwoven with the far larger ones, and they are part and parcel of each other's dynamics and raison d'etre. *Mali rat* is related to a stage of state formation that is characteristic of this part of ex-Yugoslavia, where the monopoly over the means of organized violence is still ineffectively founded upon a central plan.

2. I can not provide anything other than rough estimations. The registration records in Čitluk were destroyed, which is generally viewed as part of a war strategy focused upon destroying the territorial claims of certain segments of the population. The parish of Medjugorje has its own records, but they are said to have been destroyed as well.

3. Cf. Elias 1989: 226-227. Jonathan Haas developed a similar thought in his book *The Anthropology of War* (1990).

   For those who are not familiar with Elias's theory on civilizing processes (which is laid down in his *opus magnum, The Civilizing Process*) the following, crude summary may be of some help. Due to a wide range of 'factors', in the past thousand years more and more people in Western Europe have become ever more dependent on each other economically, socially and in other senses. As a result, they have been forced to take each other into consideration and keep their own emotions, such as rage or ten-dencies towards violence, under control. This external or social constraint has gradual-ly become virtually automatic: people's personality structure altered, and this pro-vided opportunities for further integration. It is this external or social constraint towards self-constraint, expressed in all kinds of prohibitions pertaining to the use of violence and agression, that is a consistent aspect of the argumentation.

   Central to Elias's thinking is 'figuration' or 'configuration', a concept he never bothers to define in any formal way. In order to break away from the current di-chotomic and static thinking, Elias introduced the concept, in which human figura-tions are pluralities of interdependent people who are linked to each other in numer-ous ways which they themselves realize at best only partially. Figurations have no separate existence from the individuals who together constitute them; they are neither less nor more real than these people. As he himself puts it: 'Individuals always come in figurations and figurations are always formed by individuals' (Elias and Dunning 1966: 396-397). Any social form—teachers and pupils in a classroom, card-players at a table, football players on a field, nuclear families, towns, villages, political parties, nation-states—can be understood as figurations. Figurations have dynamics of their own, which are usually only partly understood by those who form them. They result from the inherent tensions and conflicts (moves and counter-moves) between the indi-viduals who constitute the figuration. Figurations are thus in constant flux. However, their changes through time are not to be seen as the product of calculated and planned actions of (some) individuals. Rather, they must be understood as a relatively autonomous and purposeless—but nevertheless structured—developmental process. Thus, 'in the development of human figurations, yesterday's unintended social consequences are today's unintended social conditions of intentional human actions' (Goudsblom 1977: 149). These figurations are, of course, interconnected with larger ones, which follow equally blind courses, relatively independent of the objectives of their members. The more complicated the figuration, the more autonomous its development is in relation to the actions of its constituent members. The dynamics and changes of relatively small and simple figurations, in which the power balances are very unequal, can be understood to a certain extent in terms of the actions of the powerful few. (But equally, why these few act as they do can only be understood in relation to the figuration in which they are entangled.) The development of a more complex figuration, however, in which power is fragmented and dispersed over many persons, cannot be explained by focusing on certain individuals. The structure of its changes is relatively autonomous of the objectives of its members.

4. As to the relation between the shifting spheres of influence on the peripheries of polities and the occurrence of self-help and local formations of violence, see Boehm 1985; cf. also Seers *et al.* 1979.

5. The Muslims do not play a role in the story to be told here.

6. A. Djilas (1991) noted that these terms refer to small para-military groups that were first observed in the early days of Turkish rule.

7. Snakes feature in many of the sayings and proverbs of the region, symbolizing unreliability and unpredictability. Relations in Hercegovina were often described to me by way of the saying *Ne vieruj zmiji ni kad bi imala sobje strane rep* (Never trust a snake, not even if it has two tails).

8. 'Mars must be more hospitable than western Hercegovina and it is hard to imagine anybody wanting to conquer it ...' (Glenny 1992: 155).

9. It was not until the late eighties, after the decline of communism in Yugoslavia, that hesitant steps were made toward a certain extent of openness about the reign of the Partizans and the communists. It is only with the greatest reticence that A. Djilas (1991) cited the names of a few authors. Nowadays there are no longer traces of candour among authors in ex-Yugoslavia.

10. Until recently, Bosnia Hercegovina was known as the republic with the greatest firearms density and the largest military arsenal of all Yugoslavia. In addition to numerous arms and munitions plants, there were factories for tanks, various armoured vehicles, cannons, military aeroplanes and missiles, and there was hardly a village or town without its own arms and munitions depot (Wiener 1986). There were various reasons for this high concentration. After the Second World War, the Tito administration decided to transfer the military industries along the borders of Yugoslavia to safer sites further inland. With its dense forests and relatively inaccessible mountain valleys, the republic of Bosnia Hercegovina was viewed as the appropriate spot for the federal state's military arsenal. The fact that the area was rich in coal and mineral deposits promoted the further expansion of the military industry. In response to the Russian intervention in Czechoslovakia in 1968, Tito decided in 1969 to organize people's militia, making it feasible to mobilize the entire population in wartime. The *Teritorialna Odbrana* or T.O. (Territorial Defence) was set up, which not only served to support the regular army, but could also operate independently. For this purpose, in almost all towns and villages arms and munitions depots were built, which were under the supervision of local militia and where all the adults, women as well as men, played

a role. Each local community could thus function as a relatively autonomous para-military unit. Although designed to create a unified Yugoslav military powerhouse, the system contained the seeds for a highly complex internal 'total war' like the one that engulfed Bosnia and in part Croatia as well. More information about the Territorial Defence and its problematic relation to the regular federal army can be found in: Mladenović 1970; Ramet 1985; Hofwiler 1992; Wiener 1986; Remington 1979; Ross Johnson 1973 and Rusinow 1971.

11. These changes have been described in detail in Chapters Two, Three, Four and Seven.

12. Cf. Chapter Seven.

13. In 1990 Zagreb Turist reported that 19% of the total turnover in the country's tourist sector was from the devotion centre in Medjugorje.

14. *Mostarski list*, 28 August 1992.

15. The HOS (Hrvatske Obrambene Snage) is a para-military wing of the extremely militant and violence-oriented nationalist Party of the Right (*Hrvatska Stranka Prava*) led by S. Paraga. As regards its aims and methods, this party is similar to the former *Ustaša* movement in the days of World War Two. In the past, men of the Šivrić and Jerković clans had been members of a gang that covered the entire Brotnjo area and regularly attacked the (Serb) government.

16. Inquiries among the refugees from Medjugorje in Germany revealed that the parties were not in agreement. One party claimed the relative tranquility was promoted by the arrival of a group of pilgrims. The other party maintained that a group of pilgrims took advantage of the relative tranquility in Medjugorje at the time. Further investigation made it clear that up to the end of February, a group of fanatic pilgrims from Canada led by two of their own priests was in Medjugorje for more than ten days. When I questioned him over the telephone, a priest informed me that they had not noticed any traces of warfare in Medjugorje. They found it quite understandable that there were no priests in the village, and that uniformed men had blocked their way to the Mountain of the Cross 'because of hostilities'. This information reveals something of the difference in perception between villagers and pilgrims.

17. They were mainly men from Croat villages that had been 'purged' of Serbs. There were also a few relatives from East Slavonia, the children or grandchildren of former *Ustaša* members who emigrated from the region. The vengeful mentality of these emigrants in their battle against Serbs in East Slavonia—who also come from Hercegovina—has been disconcertingly described by Glenny (1992).

18. It was mainly during this period that the exodus to Germany took place.

19. The mutilations followed a fixed pattern, with more and more parts of the bodies being removed. The symbolic dynamics would undoubtedly be an informative field for further research.

20. It is said to be the same ravine where a similarly horrendous mass grave was effectuated toward the end of World War II. It is one of the many historical sites where hatred lives on for the suffering that has been inflicted. See also Chapter Seven and Epilogue.

Epilogue

Šurmanci's Secret:
A Never-Ending Story?

*'... [m]any ... fight for the freedom of opinion against
another ethnic collective.'* (Svetlana Slapšak 1993)
*'The South Slavs have ... suffered extremely from the
inability ... to produce men who are able both to conquer territory and to administer it.'* (Rebecca West
1982)

An Explosion and a Shameful Discovery

Late in the summer of 1992, just before nightfall, a loud explosion
resounded in the quiet village of Bijakovići. I was just about to get up
from the table and see what happened when the huge hands of my host,
Franjo, pushed me back in my chair. 'It is nothing ... we'll stay inside', he
said emphatically. In bed that night, I thought it over. Apparently Franjo
did not want me asking any questions. For that matter, no one in the
room had paid any attention to the explosion. It was as if everyone was
prepared for it, and then simply went about their business.

We were working on the land the next morning when I brought it up
again, but Franjo acted as if he did not hear me. It was not until the lunch
break, when I said I would go have a look in the direction of Šurmanci,
the hamlet I thought the sound of the explosion had come from, that my
landlord and friend reacted. At the end of the afternoon, he said, he would
show me what had happened.

Without a word, we drove toward Šurmanci in his old Volkswagen. I
was familiar with part of what barely deserved being called a road, for I
had been there a year before the 'war'.[1] About half way, we turned into a
side road. Unlike the first part, it was nice and smooth. We made another

119

turn and a few kilometres further we stopped at what looked like a huge parking lot in the middle of nowhere. At the bottom of the ravine to the left, the Neretva River flowed past, and in the mountainside to the right, steps had been hacked out leading to a shapeless mass of stone that lit up brightly in the setting sun. We silently climbed the partially ravaged staircase. It stopped at a plateau with the remains of a monument. 'Comrades blew up this blasted Chetnik monument', Franjo informed me with a torrent of curses. He spit with contempt on the remains and turned away. On our way back in the car, I felt the tension gather between us, and did not say a word. The road was so bad that the pipe of the cooling system broke, and when I started asking questions while he repaired it, that was when the 'bomb' burst. 'Why, why, why ... you always want to know why!' Hadn't I ever noticed that people didn't want to answer my questions about Šurmanci? (I had.) Hadn't I ever noticed that no taxi, or anyone at all, ever wanted to go to Šurmanci? (I had.) Hadn't I ever noticed that the people here all acted as if Šurmanci didn't exist? 'Look at the road. It is almost impossible to drive down that road. Everyone from around here tosses their garbage alongside the road. There are no signs telling you the way to Šurmanci. At the church, all the hamlets are listed on the big tablet—not Šurmanci. In all the guidebooks for tourists, the hamlets here are described—not Šurmanci. You can buy postcards and slides of almost every spot around here—not of Šurmanci'. Franjo concluded his tirade, alluding to my not being more perceptive, by saying, 'To us here, Šurmanci is dead ... we want to forget'.

A few days later, Father Leonard revealed a bit more of the secret. He told me people wanted to pretend Šurmanci did not exist because it reminded them of oppression, humiliation and forced labour. In the Second World War, he explained, many Serbs from the vicinity, especially from nearby Žitomislići, were killed by the local *Ustaši* and tossed into the ravine at Šurmanci. During Tito's regime, their descendants and other relatives took every opportunity to remind the Croats of what had happened. The monument at Šurmanci was the largest and most painful reminder. 'That is Šurmanci's secret', Father Leonard concluded. 'Here every village has a secret like that'.[2]

A few weeks later (I was gone by then), Medjugorje was startled by a few enormous explosions. Villagers from Žitomislići who were said to be fanatic Serbs had blown up the most crucial part of the bridge over the Neretva, destroying the most important connection between the Brotnjo plateau and Mostar. Pursued by a group of Croat *režervisti*, the people of Žitomislići fled with their families high into the mountains, where they settled in a former Muslim village now controlled by a Serb military unit. At any rate for the time being, a long tradition of violence and enmity between two rural communities in the region had come to an end.

Since the outbreak of the war in Bosnia Hercegovina in April 1992, a great deal of attention has been focused on what the underlying causes might have been. How is it possible, observers have wondered, that people who lived side by side in peace for decades on end suddenly developed such fierce animosity? The answer is often sought in the recent past: Tito's policy failed; the spectre of ethno-nationalism was revived (cf. Glenny 1992; Slapšak 1993; Anstadt 1992; Irvine 1993; Plestina 1992; Schöpflin 1993; Brey 1993; Thompson 1992; Peternel 1993; Parin 1993; Dringa 1993). Explanations of this kind certainly have their merits, but in one important respect they fail: they do not clarify why hostility was perpetuated. Šurmanci's secret and the related enmity between the people of Medjugorje and Žitomislići provide an interesting opportunity to shed more light on this aspect.

Gatekeepers and Peasants

On the east bank of the Neretva River, where numerous roads lead from the mountain villages to the age-old trade route from the sea to Mostar, there are a couple of small towns. These *vratari* (gatekeepers), as the towns and their inhabitants are called locally, were founded in the Ottoman Empire. They were small garrison strongholds that oversaw the communication between the mountain villages and the market centres along the river. The predominantly Muslim population earned a living collecting the tributes for the local authorities, maintaining law and order in their area, and charging tolls on all the traffic of passengers, goods and animals between the market centres and the peasant communities (Balić 1992; Vego 1981). In view of their functions, it is no wonder the gatekeepers were unpopular with the peasants and the merchants from the towns. They were regularly ambushed by gangs of revengeful peasants, who were however just as regularly disciplined by the garrisons. Their wealth made the gatekeepers attractive to gangs of roving bandits (Koljević 1980; Balić 1992; Wilson 1970).

Žitomislići was one of these gatekeepers: it controlled almost the entire Brotnjo plateau. Žitomislići is still associated with a winepress (*presa za*

grozdje), as the precious grape juice from the Brotnjo plateau was appro-
priated there, and the worthless peels remained behind.

When the Ottoman Empire began to waver in the latter nineteenth
century, a group of Serb rebels from Montenegro took advantage of the
opportunity to conquer the rich town of Žitomislići, banish or murder
the local population, and occupy the luxurious settlement themselves.
However, the whole area soon fell under Hapsburg rule. In their efforts to
pacify and incorporate the mainly Croat peasant population, the Hapsburgs were only too happy to use the militant Montenegrin Serbs (Soldo
1964; Vego 1981; Balić 1992). For the Croats of the Brotnjo, ever since
then Žitomislići has been a symbol of Serb oppression and exploitation.

When the Serbia-dominated Kingdom of Yugoslavia was founded in
1929, hostilities soon escalated and the region became the site of more and
more bloodshed. Groups of East Bosnian *Četnići*, originally a loosely
organized auxiliary of the national police, began to terrorize the population of the Brotnjo. With Žitomislići as their home base—and soon with
the help of *mjesni četnići* (local fighters), they would pillage the plateau.
They raped women, stole cattle, destroyed vineyards and water cisterns,
burned houses and barns to the ground, and viciously penalized any resistance (Soldo n.d.). An elderly informant from Medjugorje, a twelve-year-
old child at the time, compared those calamities to the present-day hostilities: 'Nothing has changed ... only the horses have become tanks'.

The officially authorized reign of terror of the *Četnići* evoked a Croat
counterpart: supported by nationalistic political circles from Split and the
surrounding area, Brotnjo peasants organized vigilante and resistance
groups. Medjugorje became the centre of the new *Ustaša* movement for
the Brotnjo, battling a perpetual mini-war with Žitomislići (Soldo 1964,
n.d.).

In the early years of World War Two, this regional violence formation
was incorporated into a war figuration of national proportions. Backed by
the Axis powers, the Independent State of Croatia was founded, and Bosnia Hercegovina was part of it. With the help of the para-military *Ustaša*
organization and backed sometimes by local Roman Catholic clergymen,
the young state took every opportunity to cleanse Croatia and Bosnia
Hercegovina of Serb elements.[3] In addition to forced conversions to
Roman Catholicism, mass deportations and massacres were among the
means to that end.

In Medjugorje, the *Ustaša* headquarters of the Brotnjo, 'preparations
were made for action'. Reportedly in conjunction with groups from Čapljina, Humac and Široki Brijeg, plans were made to cleanse the peripheral

122

regions of the Brotnjo. Žitomislići was high on the list in this connection. 'In the late summer of 1942, the time had come', one of my most belligerent informants told me. All the people of Žitomislići—in so far as they were not in active battle somewhere else—were taken prisoners and herded into a colossal bunker built into a cliff by the Germans. The plan to close off the entranceway and leave them there was abandoned, or so my informant told me, when a 'better' option came up. A column of lorries packed with Serb prisoners and led by Germans changed command near Žitomislići, and the Brotnjo Ustaši were now in control. They added their 'shipment' from Žitomislići and headed toward Šurmanci. There, far from the inhabited world, the prisoners were slaughtered like cattle and tossed into the ravine.

Like the other hamlets involved in atrocities of this kind, Medjugorje was severely punished. In the end, the outcome of the reprisals, later carried out by Tito's Partizans, was that the parish of Medjugorje lost about half its population and suffered considerable material losses.[4] This was not the end of it, for concealed behind official communist rhetoric, after the war Medjugorje was to go through a lengthy period of subjugation and humiliation.

Forced Labour and Humiliation

The liberation committees set up by Tito and his Partizans in World War Two to serve as local authorities in the conquered territories were not averse to the use of violence. In the post-war period as well, as the new 'civil society' was constructed, violence, intimidation and terror continued to be integral policy components (Alexander 1979; Ristić 1966). Numerous newly created official positions on the federal, national and local levels were 'awarded' to 'liberators of the people'. Formally expected to carry out party policies, in actuality they ruled as potentates whose main aim was to accumulate wealth and settle old accounts (Alexander 1979; Soldo n.d.; M. Djilas 1975).

Former Partizan commander Stojan Stojanović was the first to visit the ghost town of Žitomislići after World War Two. Together with a few other young men who were members of the same clan, he had been able to escape the heinous revenge the Ustaši took on his native village. The men had joined a Montenegrin Partizan unit. Their power and influence had mushroomed in the course of the post-war cleansing campaign in the region to eliminate the Ustaša movement. In view of their success, they were put in charge—allegedly by the party—of the administrative, economic and demographic reconstruction of Žitomislići.

Within little more than a decade, by the early sixties, it was as if a miracle had taken place in the ravaged town. Almost all the houses had been rebuilt and were now occupied by relatives of the former residents, the bridge over the Neretva had been repaired, the roads had been repaved, and a new small Orthodox church had even been built.

Whence this 'miracle'? Some sources mention considerable sums of government funding supplemented by special Soviet aid earmarked for their sorely afflicted Serb brothers (Vego 1980; Šimić 1976; Soldo 1964). In another publication (Smilan 1977), references are made to continual assistance from Serb emigrants and *Gastarbeiter*. Still another source emphasizes the energy and the Partizan mentality of the local population (Dragan 1978).

In addition to these possibly correct and relevant explanations, Soldo (n.d.) notes another point that deserves special attention here. After the war, he observes, the Brotnjo—like other regions in Bosnia Hercegovina—was carved up into a number of unofficial provinces 'ruled' by (Serb) Partizan leaders: a power constellation that was still in existence at the outbreak of the most recent warfare.[5] Every household that had been linked to the *Ustaša* movement (and that included all the Croat households in the region) had to make 'reparations' or pay off 'war debts' to the Partizan Fund, which was in actuality managed by the Serb establishment. Whoever refused to do so was accused of subversive nationalistic conduct, invariably resulting in imprisonment.[6] Stojan Stojanović and his men 'ruled' the northern section of the Brotnjo, which included Medjugorje, Bijakovići and Šurmanci. The villagers have greatly contributed to the reconstruction of Žitomislići and the prosperity of its inhabitants (Soldo n.d.).

In the late sixties, these policies made way in theory for a movement to promote 'brotherhood and unity', but in actuality only served to reinforce ethnic animosity. The state government in Sarajevo made funds available to 'promote the cultural legacy', and local authorities could submit proposals in this connection.[7] In Medjugorje, the population was confronted with this 'promotion' in the spring of 1970. It took quite a bit of prodding on my part to get a few of the villagers to tell me about it. 'A van of armed men came: *Četnići* from Žitomislići. They stopped at the crossing where Djure Šivrić's house used to be. Further down, they blocked off part of the mountain with little red flags ... Later we heard explosions, and that evening we saw that part of the mountain had been blown up. Then we had to come and work, chopping stones and carrying them away. But no one came. That is why the police from Čitluk took the people from their homes. A lot of men fled to the mountains, but when they came back home at night, the police came and took them away'.

Bit by bit, it became clear to the local people, and later to me as well, that the Četnići were building a monument for their war comrades, and that the Ustaši had to do the actual work. For almost three years, the people of Medjugorje, Bijakovići and Šurmanci did all they could to sabotage the work, but the authorities kept forcing them to do their share in building the monument. Without exception, obstruction led to arrests, which meant either paying a fine or doing a few days of forced labour (Soldo n.d.).[8]

After the unveiling ceremony on 27 April, 1973, the humiliation went on. The authorities never had trouble finding a reason to punish someone, especially considering the way the villagers were apt to act. Garbage discarded alongside the road had to be removed, potholes in the surface of the road had to be repaired, there had to be more and better parking space. There was an almost endless succession of sabotage and punishment, with annual peaks around 27 April. That was when thousands of detested Četnići would gather from far and wide in their automobiles to 'celebrate the past'; Partizan heroism and party loyalty were the main themes on these occasions. They were loud-mouthed, or so I have been told, and uncouth, and this evoked local objections, which in turn incited the authorities to do their best to 'get matters back to normal', for example by ordering villagers to clean the streets.

Toward the mid-eighties, this complex of ethnic animosity, which was what it was, faded into the background. 'It was thanks to the power of the Mother of God', said Father Leonard, though others felt it was 'thanks to the economic boom in Medjugorje that the authorities benefited from as well'. Whatever the case may be, there were no further large-scale ceremonial events near the monument.

In 1992, when the Serb-controlled state monopoly over the organized means of violence disintegrated, the hated monument near Šurmanci 'disintegrated' as well. 'But the memory lives on -- on both sides', lamented Father Leonard.

Food for Thought

Šurmanci's secret is not the only one of its kind. Up to now (mid-1994), I have been able to trace sixteen similar configurations of Serb power centres and Croat communities dominated by them.[9] There is probably a more general pattern, characteristic of western and southern Hercegovina, of ethnically based antagonism between pairs or clusters of village communities.

Why do people in the West know so little about this presumably more general pattern? How has it been kept from being observed? A partial explanation can be sought in the effective concealment strategies of the communist regime under Tito. Every effort to draw public attention to nationalistic differences was relentlessly suppressed, and any steps taken to critically scrutinize the recent past were punished by imprisonment (Balić 1992; Kideckel 1993; Ramet 1985; Hammel and Halpern 1969).[10]

This Western unawareness was not alleviated by any anthropological or ethnographic studies at the grass-roots level. In the impressive review article they wrote in 1983, Halpern and Kideckel did not mention a single publication about local political relations and processes, for the simple reason that there were none. The study of ethnicity in former Yugoslavia long remained confined to analyses of the cultural content of ethnic identity (e.g. Hammel 1969; Lockwood 1972, 1975, 1978, 1981) or focused on the politically relatively innocuous inter-state level (e.g. Beck and Cole 1981; Sugar 1980).[11] And as late as 1991, the influential Andrei Šimić[12] dismissed the phenomenon of ethno-nationalism in former Yugoslavia as 'folk ideology' (Šimić 1991). It was not until the recent warfare that anthropologists of the region became painfully aware of how selective their attention had been. Slowly the realization has begun to spread that to a large extent, the present-day hatred and atrocities are predominantly continuations on a larger scale of processes at the grass-roots level that were concealed behind the official communist rhetoric (cf. e.g. Kideckel 1993; Halpern 1993; Šimić 1993; Denich 1991, 1993; Hayden 1993; Despalatovic 1993; Ballinger 1994; Bowman 1994).

Notes to Epilogue

1. See Chapter Six, note 7.
2. People have only recently ventured to speak and write about the background of the mass graves and monuments related to what happened in the Second World War and the succeeding decades. The official versions propagated by the authorities always turn out to have an unofficial counterpart adhered to by a minority of the population that tells quite a different story (e.g. Glenny 1992; Brey 1993; Rathfelder 1992; Reissmüller 1992, 1993; Denich 1991; Soldo n.d.). Nonetheless, as I myself had to learn by experience, it remains an extremely sensitive topic. When I took pictures of the remains of the monument at Šurmanci and of the surrounding area in the summer of 1993, I was apparently observed by the police, who were Croats at the time. A few hours later, they came to where I was staying and informed me that, much to their regret, they had to confiscate my rolls of film. When I objected and said I had not photographed any classified sites, they told me *they* were now the ones who decided what was classified and what was not.
3. See also Chapters Six and Seven.
4. More information about this is given in Chapter Seven. See also Maček 1957; Craig 1988; Anonymous 1986; Soldo n.d.
5. In 1992, a source of extensive documentation material about these ethnically based hostilities in the region was brought to my attention. A journalist at *Mostarski list* in Mostar had stored a collection of documents based upon his own research in the archives of his newspaper, in anticipation of the appropriate moment to publish them. I was able to leaf through and read some of the documents, and make copies of what I felt were some very salient parts. When I wanted to continue my research in 1993, the newspaper building turned out to have been destroyed, as had almost all buildings in the city centre.
6. Almost all the young men in Medjugorje at the time had prison sentences for this reason, which they had to serve in Mostar or Sarajevo.
7. Cf. *Mostarski list*, 12 March 1968.
8. Even Father Siro, who was serving the parish at the time, had to tote stones as punishment for giving a sermon comparing the parishioners to the Jews who had to make tiles for the Egyptians.
9. This information is largely based upon talks with the regional researchers Vego and Soldo. More extensive and systematic research is definitely called for. See also note 2.
10. In addition to Stalinistic communists, most of the convicts at the notorious political prison Goli Otok (situated just behind the tourist island of Rab) were nationalists (cf. Soldo n.d.).
11. Lockwood (1978) is an exception, but his article focuses on the Muslim group in Bosnia Hercegovina, which was less controversial at the time.
12. In a 1993 publication, this same author—Šimić—does however admit that he had been short-sighted.

Bibliography

Alexander, S. (1979) *Church and State in Yugoslavia since 1945*, Cambridge: Cambridge University Press.

Anderson, B. (1992) *Long-Distance Nationalism*, Amsterdam: CASA Publications.

Anonymous (1974) *Opći šemitizam katoličke crkvu u Jugoslaviji*, Zagreb: Kršćanska Sadašnjost.

Anonymus (1986) *Hercegovina u NOB-u (II)*, Sarajevo: Berdon.

Anstadt, M. (1992) *Al mijn vrienden zijn gek*, Den Haag: BZZTôH.

Asad, T. (1983) Anthropological Conceptions of Religion: Reflections on Geertz, *Man (NS)*, 18 (3): 237-259.

Auclair, R. (1968) *Kerizinen: Apparitions en Bretagne?*, Paris: Nouvelles Editions Latines.

Bailey, F. (1969) *Stratagems and Spoils: An Anthropology of Politics*, Oxford: Blackwell.

Balić, A. (1992) *Das unbekannte Bosnien*, Wien: Böhlau.

Balikći, A. (1965) Quarrels in a Balkan Village, *American Anthropologist*, 67: 1456-1469.

Ballinger, P. (1994) The Politics of Submersion: History, Collective Memory, and Ethnic Group Boundaries, in: G. Bowman (ed.) *Antagonism and Identity in the National Idiom: The Case of Former Yugoslavia*, Oxford: Berg.

Banac, I. (1984) *The National Question in Yugoslavia: Origins, History, Politics*, Ithaca: Stale Press.

Banac, I. (1992) The Origins and Development of the Concept of Yugoslavia, in: M. van den Heuvel and J.G. Siccama (eds) *The Disintegration of Yugoslavia*, Amsterdam: Rodopi, pp. 1-22.

Barth, F. (1989) The Analysis of Culture in Complex Societies, *Ethnos*, 54 (3/4): 120-142.

Bax, M. (1976) *Harpstrings and Confessions: Machine-Style Politics in the Irish Republic*, Amsterdam: Van Gorcum.

Bax, M. (1983a) 'Us' Catholics and 'Them' Catholics in Dutch Brabant: The Dialectics of a Religious Factional Process, *Anthropological Quarterly*, 56 (4): 167-178.

Bax, M. (1983b) Religious Infighting and the Formation of a Dominant Catholic Regime in Southern Dutch Society, *Social Compass*, 32: 57-72.

Bax, M. (1985) Popular Devotions, Power and Religious Regimes in Catholic Dutch Brabant, *Ethnology*, 24 (3): 215-227. (Also published in: F. McGlynn and A. Thuden (eds) (1991) *Anthropological Approaches to Political Behavior*, Pittsburgh: University of Pittsburgh Press, pp. 273-293.)

Bax, M. (1987) Religious Regimes and State Formation: Towards a Research Perspective, *Anthropological Quarterly*, 60 (1): 1-11.

Bax, M. (1992) Saint Gerard's Wrath: Religious Power Politics in a Dutch Community, *Anthropological Quarterly*, 65 (4): 117-186.

Benthem van den Bergh, G. van (1989) *The Taming of the Great Powers*, Oxford: Blackwell.

Beevers, J. (1953) *The Sun Her Mantle*, Dublin: Mac Publications.

Bičanić, R. (1936) *Kako živi narod -- život u pasivnum krajevima*, Zagreb: ASU.

Black-Michaud, J. (1975) *Cohesive Force*, New York: St. Martin's Press.

Blais, Y.M. (1985) *500 messages à vivre*, Montréal: Le Lion.

Blecourt, W. de (1990) *Termen van Toverij*, Nijmegen: SUN.

Bloys, L. (1970) Celle qui pleure, in: J. Petit (ed.) *Oeuvres*, Paris: Oeil, pp. 111-259.

Boehm, C. (1985) *Blood Revenge: The Anthropology of Feuding in Montenegro and Other Tribal Societies*, Kansas: University of Kansas Press.

Boissevain, J. (1974) *Friends of Friends: Networks, Manipulators and Coalitions*, Oxford: Blackwell.

Boissevain, J. (1977) When the Saints Go Marching Out, in: E. Gellner and J. Waterbury (eds) *Patrons and Clients*, London: Duckworth, pp. 81-97.

Boniface, E. (1966) *Padre Pio de Pietrelcina*, Paris: N.E.L.

Boogaard, R. van den (1992) *Gewijde grond. De kwade kansen na de val van het wereldsocialisme*, Amsterdam: Meulenhoff.

Bouteiller, M. (1966) *Médicine populaire d'hier et d'aujoud'hui*, Paris: Larosse.

Bowman, G. (1994) Constitutive Violence and Rhetorics of Identity: A Comparative Study of Nationalist Movements in the Israeli-Occupied Territories and Former Yugoslavia, in: B. Kapferer (ed.) *Nationalism and Violence*, Oxford: Oxford University Press.

Božić, I. (1972) *Istorija Jugoslavije*, Beograd: Uos.

Brey, T. (1993) *Die Logik des Wahnsinns. Jugoslavien - von Tätern und Opfern*, Freiburg: Herder.

Bringa, T.R. (1993) National Categories, National Identification and Identity-Formation in 'Multinational' Bosnia, *The Anthropology of East Europe Review*, 11 (1-2): 69-77.

Brunner, E. (1986) *Medjugorje i Gospa*, Duvno: Samobar.

Brown, P. (1982) The Rise and Function of the Holy Man, in: P. Brown (ed.) *Society and the Holy in Late Antiquity*, Berkeley: University of California Press, pp. 103-153.

Bubalo, J. (1984) *Ik zie Maria*, Brugge: Tabor. (Originally: *Je vois la Vierge*, Paris: OEIL, 1984.)

Bubalo, J. (1985) *Vicka i Kraljica Mira*, Samobar: Matos.

Campbell, E. (1982) The Virgin of Guadalupe and the Female Self-Image: A Mexican Case History, in: J.J. Preston (ed.) *Mother Worship: Theme and Variations*, Chapell Hill: University of North Carolina Press, pp. 5-25.

Christian, W.A. Jr. (1972) *Person and God in a Spanish Valley*, New York: Seminar Press.

Christian, W.A. Jr. (1973) Holy People in Peasant Europe, *Comparative Studies in Society and History*, 15: 106-114.

Christian, W.A. Jr. (1984) Religious Apparitions and the Cold War in Southern Europe, in: E.R. Wolf (ed.) *Religion, Power, and Protest: The Northern Shore of the Mediterranean*, Berlin: Mouton, pp. 239-267.

Christian, W.A. Jr. (1987) Tapping and Defining New Power: The First Month of Visions at Ezquioga, July 1931, *American Ethnologist*, 14: 140-166.

Cohn, N. (1975) *Europe's Inner Demons: An Inquiry Inspired by the Great Witch-Hunt*, London: Blackwell.

Cole, J. (1981) Ethnicity and the Rise of Nationalism, in: S. Beck and J.W. Cole (eds) *Ethnicity and Nationalism in Southeastern Europe*, Amsterdam: Euromed Papers, no 14: 105-135.

Collins, R. (1990a) Violent Conflict and Social Organization: Some Theoretical Implications of the Sociology of War, *Amsterdams Sociologisch Tijdschrift*, 16 (4): 63-88.

Collins, R. (1990b) *Weberian Social Theory*, Cambridge: Cambridge University Press.

Čopić, B. (1963) *Prolom*, Rijeka: Adria Press.

Corish, P.J. (1985) *The Irish Catholic Experience*, Dublin: Gill & MacMillan.

Cozzi, E. (1910) La vendetta del sangue nelle montagne dell' alta Albania, *Anthropos*, 5: 624-687.

Craig, M. (1988) *Spark from Heaven: The Mystery of the Madonna of Medjugorje*, London: Hodder & Stoughton.

Crumrine, N.R. and E.A. Morinis (eds) (1990) *Pilgrimage in Latin America*, New York: Greenwood Press.

Cviić, C. (1982) A Fatima in a Communist Land?, *Religion in Communist Lands*, 10 (1): 4-9.

Davis, J. (1977) *People of the Mediterranean: An Essay in Comparative Social Anthropology*, London: Routledge & Kegan Paul.

Davis, J. (1984) The Sexual Division of Religious Labour in Islam and Christianity Compared, in: E.R. Wolf (ed.) *Religion, Power, and Protest: The North Shore of the Mediterranean*, The Hague: Mouton, pp. 17-51.

Dedijer, V. (1974) *Dvevnik, III*, Beograd i Sarajavo: Bana.

Dedijer, V. *et al.* (1975) *History of Yugoslavia*, New York: McGraw-Hill.

Denich, B.S (1974) Sex and Power in the Balkans, in: M.Z. Rosaldo and L. Lampshere (eds) *Women, Culture and Society*, Stanford: Stanford University Press, pp. 91-119.

Denich, B.S. (1976) Sources of Leadership in the Yugoslav Revolution: A Local-Level Study, *Comparative Studies in Society and History*, 18: 64-84.

Denich, B.S. (1991) Unbury the Victims: Rival Exhumations and Nationalist Revivals in Yugoslavia, Paper: American Anthropological Association Annual Meeting, Chicago, pp. 1-14.

Despalatovic, E. (1993) Reflections on Croatia, 1960-1992, *The Anthropology of East Europe Review*, 11 (1-2): 100-108.

Djilas, A. (1985) The Foundations of Croatian Identity, *South Slav Journal*, 8: 27-30.

Djilas, A. (1991) *The Contested Country: Yugoslav Unity and Communist Revolution, 1919-1953*, Cambridge, Mass.: Harvard University Press.

Djilas, M. (1957) *The New Class*, New York: East World.

Djilas, M. (1958) *Land Without Justice*, New York: Harcourt, Brace, Javanovich.

Djilas, M. (1973) *Memoir of a Revolutionary*, New York: Harcourt Books.

Djilas, M. (1977) *Wartime*, New York: Harcourt, Brace, Javanovich.

Djilas, M. (1980) *Druženje s Titom*, Beograd: CSA.

Djilas, M. (1983) *Rise and Fall*, New York: Harcourt Books.

Djordjević, T. (1953) *Veštica i vila u našem narodnom verovanju i predanju*, Beograd: Prošlost.

Douglas, M. (1982) The Effects of Modernization on Religious Change, *Daedalus* (winter): 1-20.

Dragan, V. (1978) *Žitomislići - Istorija i Geografija*, Sarajevo: Muk.

Drakulić, S. (1992) *Sterben in Kroatien*, Berlin: Rororo.

Driessen, H. (1990) Sacrale topografie. Ligging en betekenis van heilige plaatsen in Zuid-Spanje en Noord-Marokko, in: J. Verrips and K. Verrips (eds) *Ruimtegebruik en lichaamstaal in Europa en Noord-Afrika*, Amsterdam: Het Spinhuis, pp. 233-245.

Drobnjaković, B. (1960) *Etnologija naroda Jugoslavije*, Beograd: Naučna Knjiga.

Dubinskas, F.A. (1983) Leaders and Followers: Cultural Pattern and Political Symbolism in Yugoslavia, *Anthropological Quarterly*, 56 (2): 95-99.

Duijzings, G. (1993) Pilgrimage, Politics and Ethnicity: Joint Pilgrimages of Muslims and Christians and Conflicts Over Ambiguous Sanctuaries in Former Yugoslavia and Albania, in: M. Bax and A. Koster (eds) *Power and Prayer: Religious and Political Processes in Past and Present*, Amsterdam: VU University Press, pp. 79-91.

Dunning, E.G.; P. Murphy; and J. Williams (eds) (1973) *The Roots of Football Hooliganism: A Historical and Sociological Study*, London: Routledge & Kegan Paul.

Dupront, A. (1967) Tourisme et pèlerinage, *Communications*, Paris: OIEL.

Eade, J. and M.J. Sallnow (eds) (1991) *Contesting the Sacred: The Anthropology of Christian Pilgrimage*, London: Routledge.

Eliade, M. (1959) *The Sacred and the Profane*, New York: Harcourt.

Elias, N. (1956) Problems of Involvement and Detachment, *British Journal of Sociology*, 7 (3): 226-252.

Elias, N. (1978) *The Civilizing Process, Vol. I: The History of Manners*, Oxford: Blackwell.

Elias, N. (1982) *The Civilizing Process, Vol. II: State Formation and Civilization*, Oxford: Blackwell.

Elias, N. (1987a) *Involvement and Detachment*, Oxford: Blackwell.

Elias, N. (1987b) On Human Beings and Their Emotions: A Process-Sociological Essay, *Theory, Culture and Society*, 4: 339-361.

Elias, N. (1989) *Studien über die Deutschen*, Frankfurt am Main: Suhrkamp.

Elias, N. and E. Dunning (1986) *Quest for Excitement: Sport and Leisure in the Civilizing Process*, Oxford: Blackwell.

Engel, J. (1798) *Staatskunde und Geschichte von Dalmatien, Kroatien und Slavonien*, Halle: Zum Tor.

Estrade, J. (1899) *Les apparitions de Lourdes*, Paris: Nouvelles Éditions Latines.

Evans-Pritchard, E.E. (1956) *Theories of Primitive Religion*, Oxford: Oxford University Press.

Falconi, C. (1970) *The Silence of Pius XII*, London: Faber and Faber.

Filipović, M.S. (1951) Cincari u Bosni, *Zbornik Radova Etnografskog Instituta*, 2: 53-108.

Fine, J.V.A. Jr. (1975) *The Bosnian Church: A New Interpretation*, Boulder: Westview Press.

Fine, J.V.A. Jr. (1987) *The Late Medieval Balkans: A Critical Survey*, Ann Arbor: University of Michigan Press.

Fine, J.V.A. Jr. (1994) *The Late Medieval Balkans*, Ann Arbor: University of Michigan Press.

Firth, R. (1981) Spritual Aroma: Religion and Politics, *American Anthropologists*, 83: 582-601.

Gabriel, J. (1968) *Présence de la très Sainte Vierge à San Damiano*, Paris: Nouvelles Éditions Latines.

Gavranović, B. (1935) *Uspostava redovite katoličke hijerarhije u Bosni i Hercegovini 1881 godine*, Beograd: Filosofski Fakultet.

Gellner, E. and J. Waterbury (eds) (1977) *Patrons and Clients*, London: Duckworth.

Gelhard, S. (1992) *Ab heute ist Krieg. Der blutige Konflikt im ehemaligen Jugoslawien*, Frankfurt am Main: Fisher.

Geschiere, P. and W. van Wetering (1989) Zwarte magie in een onttoverde wereld, *Sociologische Gids*, 36: 150-154.

Gilmore, D. (1982) Anthropology of the Mediterranean Area, *Annual Review of Anthropology*, 12: 175-205.

Girard, R. (1977) *Violence and the Sacred*, Baltimore: Johns Hopkins University Press.

Glenny, M. (1992) *The Fall of Yugoslavia*, London: Penguin Books.

Goudsblom, J. (1988) Sociologie en levensbeschouwing, in: J. Goudsblom, *Taal en sociale werkelijkheid*, Amsterdam: Meulenhoff.

Goudsblom, J. (1989a) Human History and Long-term Social Process: Towards a Synthesis of Chronology and 'Phaseology', in: J. Goudsblom, E.L. Jones and S. Mennell, *Human History and Social Process*, Exeter: University of Exeter Press, pp. 11-27.

Goudsblom, J. (1989b) The Formation of Military-Agrarian Regimes, in: J. Goudsblom, E.L. Jones and S. Mennell, *Human History and Social Process*, Exeter: University of Exeter Press, pp. 79-93.

Guilhot, H. (1973) *La vraie Mélanie de la Salette*, Auxerre: Neuvelle.

Guldesen, S. (1964) *History of Medieval Croatia*, The Hague: Mouton.

Haas, J. (ed.) (1990) *The Anthropology of War*, Cambridge: Cambridge University Press.

Halpern, J.M. (1993) Introduction, *The Anthropology of East Europe Review*, 11 (1-2): 5-14.

Halpern, J.M. and D.A. Kideckel (1983) Anthropology of Eastern Europe, *Annual Review of Anthropology*, 12: 377-402.

Halpern, J.M. and E.A. Hammel (1969) Observations on the Intellectual History of Ethnology and Other Social Sciences in Yugoslavia, *Comparative Studies in Society and History*, 11: 17-26.

Halpern, J. and B. Halpern (1972) *A Serbian Village in Historical Perspective*, New York: Holt, Rinehart & Winston.

Hammel, E.A. (1968) *Alternative Social Structures and Ritual Relations in the Balkans*, Englewood Cliffs, N.J.: Prentice Hall.

Hammel, E.A. (1969) The 'Balkan' Peasant: A View from Serbia, in P.K. Bock (ed.) *Peasants in the Modern World*, Albuquerque: University of New Mexico Press, pp. 75-98.

Heidenheimer, A. (ed.) (1970) *Political Corruption: Readings of Comparative Analysis*, New York: Holt, Rinehart & Winston.

Hofwiler, R. (1992) Armeen, Milizen, Marodeure. Die kämpfenden Parteien und ihre Hintermänner - ein Übersicht, in: E. Rathfelder (ed.) *Krieg auf dem Balkan*, Reinbeck: Rowohlt, pp. 78-90.

Ilić, Z. (1974) *Hercegovina u Crkvi*, Duvno: Sveta Bastina.

Irvine, J.A. (1993) *The Croat Question: Partisan Politics in the Formation of the Yugoslav Socialist State*, Boulder: Westview Press.

Jelavich, B. (1990) *History of the Balkans*, 2 vols, Cambridge: Cambridge University Press.

Jelić, I. (1978) *Hrvatska u ratu i revolucija 1941-1945*, Zagreb: Ciral.

Jelić-Butić, F. (1983) *Hrvatska seljacka stranka, 1941-1945*, Zagreb: Ciral.

Jelić-Butić, F. (1986) *Četnići u Hrvatskoj*, Zagreb: Ciral.

Karadžic, V. (1935) *Srpski rječnik*, Beograd: Akademija Nauka.

Kertzer, D. (1988) *Ritual, Politics and Power*, New Haven: Yale University Press.

Kideckel, D.A. (1993) Editor's Note, *The Anthropology of East Europe Review*, 11 (1-2): 3-5.

Knežević, A. (1961) *Die Kroaten und Ihre Geschichte*, Essen: Oganje.

Koljević, S. (1980) *The Epic in the Making*, Oxford: Clarendon Press.

Kristo, J. (1982) Relations between the State and the Roman Catholic Church in Croatia, Yugoslavia in the 1970s and 1980s, *Occasional Papers on Religion in Eastern Europe*, Vol. 3 (3).

Krizman, B. (1980) *Pavelic izmedju Hitlera i Musolinija*, Zagreb: Ciral.

Krizman, B. (1983) *Ustaše i treči Reich, II*, Zagreb: Ciral.

Kselman, T.A. (1978) *Miracles and Prophesies: Popular Religion and the Church in Nineteenth-Century France*, Michigan: Michigan State University.

Laurentin, R. (1973) The Persistence of Popular Piety, in: A. Greeley and G. Baum (eds) *The Persistence of Religion*, New York: Baum, pp. 82-103.

Laurentin, R. (1984) *La Vièrge apparaît-elle à Medjugorje?*, Paris: OEIL.

Laurentin, R. (1985) *Verschijnt Maria in Medjugorje?*, Brugge: Tabor.

Laurentin, R. (1986) *Medjugorje récit et messages des apparitions*, Paris: Lethelieux.

Lockwood, W.G. (1972) Converts and Consanguinity: The Social Organization of Moslem Slavs in Western Bosnia, *Ethnology*, 11: 55-79.

Lockwood, W.G. (1974) Bride Theft and Social Maneuverability in Western Bosnia, *Anthropological Quarterly*, 47: 253-269.

Lockwood, W.G. (1975) *European Moslems: Ethnicity and Economy in Western Bosnia*, New York: Academic Press.

Lockwood, W.G. (1978) Social Status and Cultural Change in a Bosnian Moslem Village, *East European Quarterly*, 9: 123-124.

Lockwood, W.G. (1981) Religion and Language as Criteria of Ethnic Identity: An Exploratory Comparison, in: S. Beck and J.W. Cole (eds) *Ethnicity and Nationalism in Southeastern Europe*, Amsterdam: Euromed Papers, no 14: 71-82.

Lodge, O. (1941) *Peasant Life in Yugoslavia*, London: Seely.

Lukes, S. (1975) Political Ritual and Social Integration, *Sociology*, 9: 289-308.

Luhrmann, T.M. (1989) *Persuasions of the Witch's Craft: Ritual Magic and Witchcraft in Present-Day England*, Oxford: Blackwell.

Maček, V. (1957) *In the Struggle for Freedom*, Pittsburgh: Pennsylvania State University Press.

Macklin, B. and N. Crumrine (1973) Three North Mexican Folk Saint Movements, *Comparative Studies in Society and History*, 15: 89-105.

Mandić, D.S. (1978) *Bosnien und Herzegowina. Geschichtlich-kritische Forschungen*, 2 Tln., Chicago: Ziral.

Marmullaku, R. (1975) *Albania and the Albanians*, London: Athlone Press.

Marwick, M. (1982) Witchcraft as a Social Strain Gauge, in: M. Marwick (ed.) *Witchcraft and Sorcery: Selected Readings*, Harmondsworth: Pelican, pp. 14-30.

Mayer, A. (1966) Quasi-Groups in the Study of Complex Societies, in: M. Banton (ed.) *The Social Anthropology of Complex Societies*, London: Tavistock.

McKevitt, C. (1988) *Suffering and Sanctity: An Anthropological Study of a Saint Cult in Southern Italy*, London (unpublished Ph.D. thesis, London School of Economics).

Mennell, S. (1989a) Short-term Interests and Long-term Processes: The Case of Civilization and Decivilization, in: J. Goudsblom, E.L. Jones and S. Mennell, *Human History and Social Process*, Exeter: University of Exeter Press, pp. 93-128.

Mennell, S. (1989b) *Norbert Elias: Civilization and the Human Self-Image*, Oxford: Blackwell.

Meijers, D. (1993) The Protestant Ethic and the Spirit of Feminism: Some Food for Thought, in: M. Bax and A. Koster (eds) *Power and Prayer: Religious and Political Processes in Past and Present*, Amsterdam: VU University Press, pp. 143-159.

Mladenovic, O. (ed.) (1970) *The Yugoslav Concept of General People's Defense*, Belgrade: Med. Politika.

Moore, R.I. (1987) *The Formation of a Persecuting Society*, Oxford: Oxford University Press.

Oss, A.C. (1978) De expansie van de bisdommen in Nieuw Spanje in de zestiende eeuw, in: B.H. Slicher van Bath and A.C. Oss (eds) *Geschiedenis van Maatschappij en Cultuur*, Baarn: Ambo, pp. 172-194.

Oreć, L. (1989) *88266 Medjugorje*, Duvno: Z.U.D.

Paine, R. (1971) A Theory of Patronage and Brokerage, in: R. Paine (ed.) *Patrons and Brokers in the East Arctic*, Toronto: University of Toronto Press.

Parin, P. (1991) *Est ist Krieg und wir gehen hin. Bei den jugoslawischen Partisanen*, Berlin: Rowohlt.

Parin, P. (1993) Woher dieser Hass?, *Die Tageszeitung* (16-12-1993).

Peternel, N. (1993) *Voorheen Joegoslavië. Achtergronden van de Balkanoorlog*, Amsterdam: Balans.

Petranović, B. (1963) Aktivnost rimokatoličkog klera protiv sredjivanja prilika u Jugoslavii, *Istorija XX veka zbornik radova*, Beograd: Akademija Nautika, pp. 263-313.

Petrovich, M. (1972) Yugoslavia: Religion and the Tension of a Multinational State, *East European Quarterly*, 6 (1): 118-135.

Pina-Cabral, J. de (1986) *Sons of Adam, Daughters of Eve: The Peasant World View of the Alto Minho*, Oxford: Oxford University Press.

Pleština, D. (1992) *Regional Development in Communist Yugoslavia: Success, Failure, and Consequences*, Boulder: Westview Press.

Quaestio (1979) *Quaestio Hercegoviniensis*, Duvno: Z.O.D.

Ramet, P. (1984) Yugoslavia and the Threat of Internal and External Discontent, *Orbis*, 28 (1): 109-120.

Ramet, P. (1985a) Factionalism in Church-State Interaction: The Croatian Catholic Church in the 1980s, *Slavic Review*, 44 (2): 298-315.

Ramet, P. (ed.) (1985b) *Yugoslavia in the 1980s*, Boulder: Westview Press.

Rathfelder, E. (ed.) (1992) *Krieg auf dem Balkan*, Hamburg: Rororo.

Reissmüller, J.G. (1992) *Der Krieg vor unserer Haustür*, Stuttgart: DVA.

Reissmüller, J.G. (1993) *Die bosnische Tragödie*, Stuttgart: DVA.

Remington, R.A. (1979) Balkanization of the Military: Party, Army and People's Militias in Southern Europe, in: K.E. Naylor (ed.) *Politics and Modernization in Southeastern Europe*, Boulder: Westview Press, pp. 21-41.

Rheubottom, D. (1976) The Saint's Feast and Skopska Crna Goran Social Structure, *Man (N.S.)*, 11: 18-34.

Rhodes, A. (1973) *The Vatican in the Age of the Dictators 1922-1945*, London: Hodder & Stoughton.

Ristić, D.N. (1966) *Yugoslavia's Revolution of 1941*, London: University Park Press.

Ross Johnson, A. (1973) Yugoslav Total National Defense, *Survival*, 15 (4): 54-58.

Rupčić, I. (1937) *Entstehung der Franziskaner Pfarreien in Bosnien und Herzegowina. Studien zur historischen Theologie*, Bresslau: Aram.

Rupčić, L. (1983) *Gospina ukazanja u Medjugorju*, Samobor: Matoš.

Rusinow, D. (1980) The Yugoslav Concept of All National Defense, *American Universities Field Staff Reports*, Southeast Europe Series, no. 19 (Kansas).

Rusinow, D. (1982) *The Yugoslav experiment 1948-1974*, London: M.S.P.C.

Rynne, 8. (1965) *The Third Session*, New York: Farrar, Strauss & Giroux.

Sadasnjost, K. (1974) *Opči semitizam katoličke crkve u Jugoslaviji*, Zagreb: Kršćanska S.

Sallnow, M. (1987) *Pilgrims of the Andes: Regional Cults in Cusco*, Washington: Smithsonian Institution Press.

Satriani, L and M. Meligrana (1982) *Il Ponte di San Giacomo*, Milano: Rizzoli.

Schmidt, S. *et al.* (eds) (1977) Friends, Followers, and Factions: A Reader in Political Clientelism, Berkeley: University of California Press.

Schöpflin, G. (1993) *Politics in Eastern Europe*, Oxford: Blackwell.

Scott, J. (1970) Corruption, Machine Politics, and Political Change, in: Heidenheimer, A. (ed.) *Political Corruption: Readings of Comparative Analysis*, New York: Holt, Rinehart & Winston, pp. 549-564.

Seers, D. *et al.* (eds) (1979) *Underdeveloped Europe*, Sussex: Harvester Press.

Šimić, A. (1967) The Blood Feud in Montenegro, *Kroeber Anthropological Society Papers*, 1: 83-95.

Šimić, A. (1991) Obstacles to the Development of a Yugoslav National Consciousness: Ethnic Identity and Folk Culture in the Balkans, *Journal of Mediterranean Studies*, 1(1): 18-37).

Šimić, A. (1993) The First and Last Yugoslav: Some Thoughts on the Dissolution of a State, *The Anthropology of East Europe Review*, 11 (1-2): 14-21.

Škaljić, A. (1957) *Turcizmi u narodum gororu i narodnoj književnosti Bosne i Hercegovine*, Sarajevo: Bilten Instituta.

Skendi, S. (1967) Crypto-Christianity in the Balkan Area Under the Ottomans, *Slavic Review*, 26: 227-246.

Slapšak, S. (1993) *Joegoslavië, weet je nog*, Amsterdam: Mets.

Smilan, I. (1977) *Dokumenti*, Sarajevo: Muk.

Soldo, J. (1964) *Čitluk i Brotnjo: Istorija*, Zagreb: Privredni Vjesnik.

Soldo, J. (n.d.) *Mali rat u Brotjnu* (manuscript).

Spier, F. (1990) Religie in de mensheidsgeschiedenis. Naar een model van de ontwikkeling van religieuze regimes in een lange-termijnperspectief, *Amsterdams Sociologisch Tijdschrift*, 16 (4): 88-123.

Spier, F. (1992a) *Religious Regimes in Peru: Religion and State Development in a Long-term Perspective and their Effects in the Andean Village of Zurite*, Amsterdam: Amsterdam University Press.

Spier, F. (1992b) The Damaging Abuse of Attending Mass in Hacienda Chapels: On Rivalling Religious Regimes and State Development in Eighteenth-Century Peru, in: M. Bax and A. Koster (eds) *Faith and Polity: Essays on Religion and Politics*, Amsterdam: VU University Press, pp. 153-173.

Spier, F. (1993) 'Civilisation Theory and Environmental Problems', Lecture held at Conference on 'Social Functions of Nature', Chantilly, France, 8-12 March.

Spier, F. (1994) *San Nicolas de Zurite: Religion and Daily Life of a Peruvian Andean Village in a Changing World* (manuscript).

Stanojević, B. (1989) *Crvena Gospa iz Medjugorja*, Beograd: Panpublik.

Stanojević, G. (1955) *Crna Gora u Doba Vladike Danila*, Četinje: Obod.

Starčević, A. (1941) *Misli i pogledi*, Zagreb: Ciral.

Stirrat, R. (1984) Sacred Models, *Man (NS)* 19: 199-215.

Sugar, P.F. (ed.) (1980) *Ethnic Diversity and Conflict in Eastern Europe*, Santa Barbara: ABC-Clio.

Swaan, A. de (1994) De staat van wandaad. Over de vervagende grenzen tussen oorlogvoering en misdaadbestrijding, in: A. de Swaan, *Twee stukken*, Amsterdam: Het Spinhuis, pp. 1-14.

Tanner, M. (1988) Holy Visions Anger Bishop, *The Independent* (22-11-1988).

Taussig, M. (1987) *Shamanism, Colonialism and the Wild Man: A Study in Terror and Healing*, Chicago: Chicago University Press.

Tentori, T. (1982) An Italian Religious Feast: The Fujenti Rites of the Madonna dell'Arco, Naples, in: J.J. Preston (ed.) *Mother Worship: Theme and Variations*, Chapel Hill: University of North Carolina Press, pp. 95-119.

Thoden van Velzen, H.U.E. and W. van Wetering (1987) Herinneringen die rondspoken: Het verleden in een Afro-Surinaamse samenleving, *Sociologisch Tijdschrift*, 14: 407-437.

Thoden van Velzen, H.U.E. and W. van Wetering (1988) *The Great Father and the Danger: Religious Cults, Material Forces, and Collective Fantasies in the World of the Surinamese Moroons*, Dordrecht/Providence: Foris Publications.

Thomas, K. (1971) *Religion and the Decline of Magic: Studies in Popular Beliefs in Sixteenth- and Seventeenth-Century England*, London: Tavistock.

Thompson, M. (1992) *A Paper House: The Ending of Yugoslavia*, London: Vintage.

Tomasevich, J. (1955) *Peasants, Politics and Economic Change in Yugoslavia*, Stanford: Stanford University Press.

Tomasevich, J. (1969) Yugoslavia During the Second World War, in W. Vučinich (ed.) *Contemporary Yugoslavia*, Berkeley: California University Press.

Tomasevich, J. (1975) *The Chetniks*, Stanford: Stanford University Press.

Turner, V. and E. Turner (1978) *Image and Pilgrimage in Christian Culture*, New York: Columbia University Press.

Vego, M. (1981a) *Historija Brotnja od najstarijih vremena do 1878 godine*, Čitluk: Alba.

Vego, M. (1981b) *Historija Brotnja*, Čitluk: Svjetlost.

Vlahović, P. and V. Dančetović (1960/1961) Prilog proučavanju žena u krvnoj osveti, *Glasnik Etnografskog Instituta*, 9: 9-10.

Vučinich, W. (1969) Interwar Yugoslavia, in: W. Vučinich (ed.) *Contemporary Yugoslavia*, Berkeley: California University Press.

Vuksan, D. (1951) *Petar I Petrović Njegoš i Njegova Doba*, Cetinje: Narodna Kniga.

Vissers, S. (1989) *Tussen kerk en kapel. Over een heilige priester en zijn vereerders in hedendaags Portugal*, Nijmegen (mimeo).

Weingrod, A. (1968) Patrons, Patronage and Political Parties, *Comparative Studies in Society and History*, 10: 377-400.

Weingrod, A. (1977) Patronage and Power, in: E. Gellner and J. Waterbury (eds) *Patrons and Clients in Mediterranean Societies*, London: Duckworth.

West, R. (1982) [1940] *Black Lamb and Grey Falcon: A Journey through Yugoslavia*, New York: Penguin Books.

Wiener, F. (1986) *Die Armeen der neutralen und blockfreien Staaten Europas*, Vienna: Carl Überreuter.

Wilson, D. (1970) *The Life and Times of Vuk Stefanivic Karadzic 1787-1864*, Oxford: Clarendon Press.

Wilson, S. (1989) *Feuding, Conflict and Banditry in Nineteenth-Century Corsica*, Cambridge: Cambridge University Press.

Wilterdink, N. (1992) Inleiding, in: H. Franke, N. Wilterdink and C. Brinkgreve (eds) *Alledaags en ongewoon geweld, Amsterdam Sociologisch Tijdschrift*, 18 (3): 7-13.

Wolf, E.R. (1966) Kinship, Friendship, and Patron-Client Relations in Complex Societies, in: M. Banton (ed.) *The Social Anthropology of Complex Societies*, London: Tavistock, pp. 1-20.

Wolf, E.R. (ed.) (1991) *Religious Regimes and State-Formation: Perspectives from European Ethnology*, New York: SUNY Press.

Žanic, Mons. Pav. (1990) *Medjugorje*, Mostar: Šetalište JNA 18.

Zimdars-Swartz, S.L. (1991) *Encountering Mary: From La Salette to Medjugorje*, Princeton: Princeton University Press.